Just This Side of Heaven

*Penny's story,
a heartwarming journey
of love and devotion*

Timothy Glass

Foreword by Cathy Perry Glass

Platinum Paw Press

Just This Side of Heaven
Timothy Glass

© Copyright Timothy Glass, 2008

Cover by Toby Mikle
Front Cover photography of Penny by Cathy Perry Glass
Back Cover photography of Timothy Glass by Cathy Perry Glass

Photo of Penny, Tyler, and Panda © Kim Jew Photography.

THERE YOU'LL BE (FROM "PEARL HARBOR")
Words and Music by Diane Warren
© 2001 REALSONGS (ASCAP)
All rights reserved. Used by Permission of ALFRED PUBLISHING CO., INC.

Platinum Paw Press
Visit our website www.platinumpawpress.com

Set in Perpetua
Book Design by Daniel Middleton
www.scribefreelance.com

Library of Congress Control Number: 2008928047
ISBN 978-0-9817067-1-9

Printed in the United States of America

Acknowledgments

AS ALWAYS, TO MY WIFE CATHY. Thank you for the gift of your love, your support, and your outlook on life. Without your understanding, this book, as well as the others, would never be more than an idea. To Lynn, my honorary mom for always being there and loving our beagles. Mostly, thank you for loving me and being a mom when you didn't have to be. To Dr. H, for providing the best care for our beagles and support for us. To Susan, my proof editor. Thank you for all that you do when my eyes seem to fail me.

To Penny, the beagle, and all the pups at the bridge until we meet again,
Godspeed.
Penny the Beagle
April 15, 1996–October 19, 2007

Contents

Foreword   i

Beaglehood   xi

Just This Side of Heaven   1

Our Story   2

Pick a State, Any State   9

Bound for New Mexico   21

Penny and Panda   29

Prairie Dogs, Jaws, and Thunderstorms   33

The Our House   40

Here Comes the Beagle, I Mean, Bride   44

Beagle Partners in Crime   51

Every Beagle Has a Season   65

Sleepytown Beagles   72

The Pattern   83

Furkids Amongst Us   89

Trip of Hope   98

Road Trip   101

October 18th   112

It's Time to Go   116

Contents

Penny's Journey 123

The Dash 129

The Unexplained 133

Day by Day 139

Thoughts of Guilt 147

Shadows and Memories 151

Epilogue 153

Foreword

WHEN I CLOSE MY EYES, I can still feel her puppy breath and her soft fur upon my cheek as I brought her home for the very first time. She wiggled and snuggled up against my neck, wondering, I'm sure, what happened to her mama. She started her new life with me with nothing more than the bag of food the breeder sent us home with and a collar and leash—bright pink, which would become her signature color.

I found her in The Boston Sunday Globe. The ad said, "Beagle puppies, $250." I called the phone number, and a man told me there were two female puppies left, although he was thinking about keeping one of them. He gave me directions to where they were, about 45 minutes away and half way to Cape Cod.

It was a warm Sunday afternoon in June. The man brought the two remaining puppies out into the sunlit yard. He then picked one up and said this was the one he was going to keep. That left one tiny ball of black fur with long ears as soft as velvet. I knew at that moment that she was mine and I happily wrote a check. I didn't know it at the time, but as I write this there is no doubt in my mind that I got the pick of the litter.

After much debate over the perfect name, I called her Penny—Pretty Penny, officially.

Penny's first bed was a cardboard box lined with towels and carefully placed beside my bed. It broke my heart to hear her cry when I put her in it. Pretty soon she was curled up in the bed next to me.

She was a wonder to me. I was amazed by how tiny she was. Her body was no bigger than my size 6 tennis shoes, and her little head was only as big as a tennis ball. When we went out to play in the front grass, Penny's black coat gleamed in the sunlight as she scampered about. I did not know that those tiny legs could run so fast, and it wasn't long before I determined that I had to get into shape or keep her on a leash!

Penny taught me many things on our journey together. One of the first was that puppy teeth are razor sharp and that hands should be kept out of their way at all times. It took me a while to learn this. Although time has faded them, I still can see the tiny scars; little trophies of the times she was quicker than me.

Penny grew quickly. I watched as her head and ears changed from black to a lovely reddish tan and she got the same color ticking, like freckles, on her white legs and paws. Her brown eyes, so clear and bright, didn't miss a thing. No squirrel or other critter that dared to venture into our backyard escaped her watchful eye. Best of all, Penny had the most beautiful smile. Soon I was finding her baby teeth on the floor and buying her a new, bigger collar. By now, Penny had a proper bed, and I loved to see her curled up in sleep. Sometimes she would sleep with her head hanging over the edge, as if it was just too much trouble to climb all the way in before falling asleep. I have a picture of her like that. It is one of my favorites and still hangs on the refrigerator to this day.

Sweet girl that she was, she never chewed on the cabinets or the furniture. I let her have the run of the downstairs while I was at work. I put a baby gate up to keep the upstairs off limits. However, in my haste to get out the door one day when I was running late, I forgot to put it at the bottom of the stairs. Thus, Penny taught me rule number two: never leave the closet door open.

When I arrived home that evening, I realized what I had done, or, I should say, not done. I went upstairs and everything appeared to be fine at first glance. Then I saw the damage. My shoes. Three of them lay strewn about the room in varying stages of destruction. And, did she chew up a matched pair plus another for good measure? No, of course not. She chose a shoe from three different pairs. I wasn't sure if Penny didn't like my taste in shoes or if she just thought I needed some new ones. In any case, it was my fault for forgetting to put the gate up, so I couldn't be mad at her.

At about the age of six months, the vet recommended that Penny be spayed. I was nervous about the surgery, partly because of the risks of anesthesia but also because I had to leave her there overnight. However, she came through the operation just fine. I brought her home with the dreaded "lampshade" collar, just in case she tried to lick or chew her stitches. They didn't seem to bother her, so I thought it was safe to leave the big, cone-shaped collar off. It was, until two or three days before the stitches were to be taken out. I came home and discovered that Penny had removed all but two of them herself!

Around this same time, I noticed the beginning of a new phase. Maybe it was the memory of the day she demolished my shoes or just another phase of puppyhood, but suddenly the stuffed toys were no longer stuffed. I think the goal was to get the squeaker out. Penny would chew and shake fiercely until mountains of cottony, white stuffing drifted throughout the house. I'm not sure how they do it, but the amount of filling that comes out of a stuffed baby is proportionately greater than the size of the baby itself. I tried to re-stuff them, but she just took it out again, so I left her with the empty fur shells to play with.

A similar fate awaited any paper, cardboard, or plastic that Penny was able to get her paws on. Gifts for her birthday and holidays were usually cast aside in favor of the box or bag they arrived in. The bathroom wastebasket was a treasure trove to Penny, as it was a great source of tissues just waiting to be shred.

It didn't take long before I was tired of picking up pieces of soggy tissue. I went out and bought a new wastebasket. This one had a dome-shaped lid that swung back and forth, and you simply pushed it open to put the trash in. When I brought it home Penny inspected it carefully. Within a matter of minutes, she learned that she could take her nose and push it open. This was my next lesson (rule number three): never try to outsmart a beagle.

When she was outside, Penny's favorite pastime was digging. The yard resembled a minefield with its random holes dotting the landscape. I tried burying treats under the deck in order to get her to dig there, where someone was less likely to step in a hole and injure an ankle. Remember rule number three (above): never try to outsmart a beagle. Not only did she dig up the treats that I buried for her, she also unearthed the bulbs I had carefully planted along the side of the house.

All the kids in the neighborhood knew and loved Penny. I'm not sure how, since I didn't even know all of them, or their names, but they would ring the doorbell and ask if they could play with her. I would send her out in the backyard with them. I sometimes felt like the neighborhood babysitter, but the kids were always well behaved and Penny loved all the attention. I used to tell people that she had more friends than I did. They thought I was joking but it was really true!

I loved having Penny in my life. The best part of my day was coming home to her smiling face and wagging tail. It was always the same enthusiastic greeting. It didn't matter if I had been gone for a few minutes or all day. She didn't care what I looked like or if I was having a bad hair day. There she would be, watching and waiting faithfully at the window.

I told Penny my secrets. She listened, sometimes resting her head on my lap as I petted her. Other times, she tilted her head to one side or the other as though helping me to consider the options. When I went through a very difficult breakup, she let me bury my face in her fur and cry, and then kissed away my tears.

Penny and I both loved the sun. I loved to sit in a sunny spot with a book and Penny curled up beside me. When the weather was nice, she would lie out on the back deck and enjoy the warmth of the sun's rays.

As time went on, Penny grew slightly taller than the acceptable 15 inches for a beagle. She held her head high and I called her my regal beagle. She was calm and took things in stride. If she was left on the other side of a door, she did not bark or scratch. And if the door was even slightly ajar, she would not push it open. Penny waited patiently, knowing that she would be missed and the door would soon be opened wide for her.

Penny loved to be petted. One of my nicknames for her was "Pet Me Penny," and I used to tell her that she was a "petaholic." She would sit for as long as anyone would pet her. She never tired of being petted. However, as sweet and loving as Penny was, she was also very independent and definitely had the stubbornness that beagles are known for.

One day, as we were getting ready to go for a walk, Penny managed to slip out the front door without her leash. I called and called to her to come to me but she would not. She pranced ahead of me on the sidewalk. With her head up, she occasionally looked back to see if I was keeping up. Penny, like the child who cries,

"Look, Mom, no hands!" seemed to be saying, "Look, Mom, no leash!" I was extremely nervous with her loose and decided to see if I could get us home via a shortcut. Penny knew the route of our daily walk. As she was about to cross the street, I called to her and turned the corner, rather than crossing the street as we usually did. She turned back and rounded the corner with me. We arrived home safely a few moments later. While I was filled with an enormous sense of relief, Penny was just as happy as could be and very proud of walking herself around the neighborhood. I felt as though she was trying to tell me that she was a big girl now.

Winter arrived in New England, and so did the snow. The backyard disappeared under mountains of white fluffy snow. Penny loved it! She ran through it, she jumped in it, she stuck her head in it and came up with snow on her nose. It was a reminder to me to find the joy in everyday things.

I worried that Penny might be lonely during the day while I was at work. I did have a lady who came in at lunchtime and took her for a walk, but that only gave her company for about 30 minutes out of the day. I decided to get another dog.

Since Penny was such a great companion, I decided to get another beagle. I called the breeder that I adopted Penny from in December. It turned out that Penny's beagle parents were due to have another litter in early January. There were eight puppies in the litter. When they were about three or four weeks old I went to see them. I chose the smallest puppy; she was quiet and gentle (or so I thought, but that's a different story). A few weeks later, I brought her home and that is how Penny got her sister, Panda.

When I got Penny, I never would have imagined that 30 pounds could make such a difference in my life. Penny gave me great joy and a few scares along the way. She brought a tremendous amount of love into my life and taught me that true love is unconditional and lives in your heart forever.

I also didn't know very much about beagles. My love for them is one of those things in my life that does not have a logical explanation. I had always loved them and wanted one, although I couldn't give you a reason why. Once I had Penny, I started reading everything I could about beagles. I also found a wonderful group of beagle lovers on the Internet. They were (and still are) a great resource for advice, support, and sharing our beagles' antics. Although most of us have never met face-to-face, we've shared laughter and tears and offered prayers up for one another in difficult times. We have celebrated new additions and mourned the passing of our beloved fur children when they have left us.

This is where I learned about things like reverse sneezing and pill pockets. It's also the place where I learned that I am not the only one who has more beagle beds than beagles, and that it's OK.

This is also the place where I met a wonderful man, Timothy Glass, who, today, is my wonderful husband and a great beagle dad. The rest of the story is his to tell.

—**Cathy Perry Glass**

Beaglehood

BEAGLEHOOD FOR ME BEGAN at an early age. I was 17 years old at the time, and I was driving to school one morning with my high school sweetheart. The traffic was extremely heavy that morning as my old truck neared a curve in the highway. There before us was a line of commuters honking and dodging a small object in the middle of the road. The object was a puppy—a very confused, scared beagle puppy at that—who was attempting to navigate his way through the sea of heavy morning traffic. Going the wrong way against the flow of traffic, I might add. I stopped, put on my emergency flashers, and jumped out of the truck with no regard to my own safety. I suppose I was simply giving morning commuters another level of challenge.

They must have loved the entertainment the young puppy and I provided, since the puppy and I got lots of horn honks. I think there were even a few motorists that cheered out their windows— well, okay, they were yelling at us, to be honest. After about ten minutes and several near misses from front bumpers, I managed to grab the puppy up in the safety of my arms and carry him back to my truck.

As I arrived at school that morning, my high school sweetheart was able to go to class. I, on the other hand, had my hands full with my newly found friend, the beagle puppy I had just rescued. I took him to my first class, and for some reason the teacher was not amused in the least. I think it was due to the fact that the puppy managed to commandeer the class right out from under her. I honestly think that if the beagle had had any knowledge of American literature, the teacher would have lost the battle.

Instead, the next thing I remember was sitting in the principal's office. He gave me the option of calling animal control, having the puppy removed, and then allowing me to go back to class. That was no option in my mind. So, with the meanest "I am principal" look on his face, we had a stare down. I was not backing down. For God's sake, it wasn't as if I had come to school with an AK-47 assault weapon in my arms. I had simply rescued a cute, cuddly beagle puppy. I think the straw that broke the camel's back was when I sat the little beagle on his desk and he walked over to a stack of papers and relieved himself on them. At that point, the principal picked up the phone. I am sure that if we would have had speed dial back in those days, my mother's number would have been first on the list. Nonetheless, I had my very first beagle, which I named Toby.

Later in life, when I became an adult and no longer had to deal with principals, I adopted a six-week-old female beagle who I named Chelsea. But it wasn't until I adopted my second female beagle that my school days came back to haunt me.

I called her Brandy. She was the runt of the litter and the only female; she far surpassed the definition of cute. However, she became sickly and unable to eat by herself a few days later. I was never quite sure why, but, as it happens, the vet later speculated that she might have been weaned too young. According to my vet, her only chance of survival hinged on me giving her round-the-clock care. I had to take a tiny syringe and inject fluid into her mouth every two hours, along with her meds. So I set my alarm clock, and every two hours I was up warming broth and feeding her to keep her hydrated.

It wasn't until the following morning that I knew I had a problem. I had to be at work. I figured I was older now and thus had more experience under my belt. After all, I had my school days and the principal as a reference, per se. I packed up Brandy, along with her broth and meds, and off we went to work. Fortunately, it was wintertime; so, over the next couple of days, I wore my jacket to work, even inside the office, telling everyone I was cold. If I heard anyone approaching my office, I would put Brandy inside my jacket, out of sight. On our second day, as she gained more strength, she would make little puppy noises under my jacket, which did present some problems with other employees when they heard them. However, I just explained that my stomach was growling. Three days after Brandy took sick, she began eating on her own again and no longer needed to be smuggled into work with me.

I survived their chewing stages, such as when Brandy decided to take up electrical work and completely unwired my boat trailer, which was parked in the yard—all 24 feet of it. She then managed to chew up the phone connections into my house several times. Brandy, at some point, began a tool collection unbeknownst to me. It seemed that every time a repairman came to my house, Brandy quickly became their best friend. However, what she was really after was their tools. Each time a repairman left, I would find brightly colored tools in her doghouse. Once I realized this, I checked her doghouse before letting them leave, which saved me from having to call them back to retrieve their tools.

Both Chelsea and Brandy lived out their lives with me until they passed on at the ages of 13 and 12, respectively. The experiences gained in these early stages of my beaglehood prepared me for the beagles to come later on in my life. These years were charting the course for my life with beagles.

Just This Side of Heaven

*A*N ORANGE GLOW FILLED the morning sky, like it had every morning, as the sun began its ascent upward to greet a new day. As always, it was nature's promise as to what was to follow.

I walked through the mist as the long shadows of morning danced beside me. This October morning had a chill to it beyond the light New Mexico desert breeze. I turned, out of habit, looking for you. Each morning you were always by my side, tracing my footsteps, no matter what the weather was like, no matter how early it was, you were there with me. Today was different, however. You were no longer beside me like you were before; you were just this side of heaven.

Our Story

MY STORY AND JOURNEY with Penny began just shortly after the loss of my three-year-old beagle, Ms. Beamer. Beamer was a beautiful 13" purebred beagle who loved to play. Bred for the show ring, she, for whatever reason, found the show ring not to her liking. Once in the ring, beagles are to carry their tails up. Not Ms. Beamer, however; she would carry her tail up until the moment she stepped into the ring, when her tail would come down between her legs. The breeder allowed me to adopt her; but if you want the honest truth, Beamer adopted me and my eight-year-old male beagle, Gunner. Beamer took over the household from the moment she put her first paw print in the house.

Shortly after I adopted her, I was hit by an uninsured drunk driver and almost killed. Once I was allowed to come home, it was Beamer who stayed by my side every moment. In fact, once I learned to walk again after my injuries, it was Beamer who took each step with me. In my effort to be independent after the wreck, I fell several times. I had lost all feeling in both legs due to nerve damage. Unable to get myself back up until the feeling in my legs would return, Beamer would lay by my side, refusing to leave me. Even after I learned to walk without falling, Beamer was always by my side. Three nights before her death, she climbed into my lap and looked deeply into my eyes. As I petted her, I talked to her as I would my best friend and asked her if she could please help me find that special woman I never seemed to be able to find on my own.

Three days later, I had a doctor's appointment in town. Like always, I put both Gunner and Beamer outside on the large covered porch where they would stay, unless they needed to go out into the fenced yard. When I returned, there was a note attached to my gate from the village animal control stating that my female beagle had been killed. After calling everywhere and talking to a few of my neighbors, I learned that Beamer had been out playing in our yard, next to my fence. My one neighbor told me that she noticed Beamer had poked her head under the fence and two large dogs on the other side tugged at her until they pulled her into their yard. After that, they killed her by mauling her and breaking her neck.

I was devastated after her death, to say the least. While I still had my eight-year-old male beagle, the death of Beamer cut deeply within. I am sure that for many, the bond and deep devotion between dog and man eludes them. I think it was Gandhi who once said a country could be measured by how it treats its animals. I truly feel the measure of a man or woman can be said to be the same.

So with Ms. Beamer gone, Gunner and I were once again bachelors, with not even a female beagle to balance the scales of maleness in our household. Nonetheless, that was about to change. A friend of mine added a short post about Ms. Beamer's death to a beagle list on the Internet that I belonged to. My inbox exploded with condolences. I never answered any of them, except one. Why? I can't explain—even to this

4

day, it is still a mystery. Her name was Cathy. Cathy lived in Norwood, Massachusetts, with her two female beagles, Penny, age three—the same age as Ms. Beamer at the time of her death—and Panda, age two. Each day, Cathy would email to check on both Gunner and me. While I think she was more interested in how Gunner was doing, I found myself looking forward to her emails.

As a sideline, I created websites; so I asked Cathy if it would be all right if I created one for Penny and Panda, a sort of home on the web, per se. Cathy was happy to send me a few photos of her two beagle girls. As a bonus, she just happened to toss one of herself in the package. One day I arrived home to find a package full of photos of Penny and Panda that I would be able to scan for their website. At the very bottom was a photo of Cathy. She was beautiful, to say the least. After several months of emails, phone calls, and photo exchanges, electronically bouncing from the East Coast to the West Coast and vice-versa, we had ourselves a long distance relationship.

It was Cathy who called me one day and asked if she could fly out to New Mexico to meet me, face to face. The fact is, I think I speak for every man in America (especially after seeing the movie, *Fatal Attraction*) when I say I was chicken! Cathy and I had emailed and talked for hours on the phone. However, somewhere in the back of my mind was this little voice asking me what if this lady was secretly...well, you know...a nut job. I finally agreed she could make a short trip out here.

After Cathy made several trips to New Mexico to visit Gunner and me, I can honestly say, for the first time in my life, I fell in love for all the right reasons. I really got to know her, and I think that made all the difference in the world.

However, it was now my turn to make the trip back to Norwood, Massachusetts, and meet Cathy's two beagles, Penny and Panda, for the first time. It was love at first sight—for me anyway. I fell in love with Cathy's two beagles. However, as with many relationships, even between men and women, love can be one-sided. When I stepped into Cathy's house for the first time, one would have thought I had just broken into the house and was about to cart off all the family's most prized heirlooms—or a can of kibble. Panda set off howling and would not stop; well, that's not exactly accurate, as there were split-second hesitations for a growl or two, and even a few snarls. All the while, the hair on her back was standing on end. I set down my suitcase and got down on the floor, thinking maybe that would help matters. Not hardly. From Panda's point of view, I was now just a smaller version of the man who walked in the door a few minutes ago. Therefore, the pitch of her bark was not equivalent to my height at all. No, in fact, Panda assumed I was now encroaching closer into her sacred beagle territory. Penny was different. While Panda barked first and judged later, Penny reserved the right to pass judgment until later.

The following morning Penny refused to eat her breakfast. Unlike most beagles who eat anything and everything (edible or not), Penny could be very finicky about what she would eat. I picked up her bowl and hand fed her, which Penny loved. I was never sure if it was the added attention I was providing her or what, but we seemed to begin our bonding that instant. Oddly, from that moment on, Penny would always walk close to my left side, just as Ms. Beamer had done after my wreck. When I would go up or down Cathy's stairs, Penny would take each step with me, always looking to make sure she knew where

I was. In a way, I believe Penny was stepping into the paw prints of Ms. Beamer for me.

Although Penny, being a full 15" beagle, was much larger in stature than Beamer, they were both tri-colored and purebred; and those were about the only similarities between them. When Cathy and I would take the beagles for a walk, I couldn't help noticing Penny's stride when she walked or trotted beside us. In my life of beagle ownership, never have I ever seen a beagle with such a remarkable stride. It is hard for me to describe it other than to say that Penny had such an air of assurance and independence with each step she took, all the while holding her head up with such pride.

I enjoyed my visits to New England, and I am sure Cathy enjoyed her stay in the southwest. Nonetheless, soon Cathy and I became tired of our long-distance relationship and decided we needed to pick one state to reside in.

Pick a State, Any State

CATHY AND I HAD decided, or at least Gunner and I thought she had decided, that we were to move to Norwood. After all, Gunner and I had lived back there with Cathy, Penny, and Panda for nine months. Besides, Gunner had some really great treasures buried in her backyard. Not to mention his favorite pastime, which was to chase Bradley, the snow-white kitty cat that lived two doors down, whenever he wandered into the backyard. Bradley loved to egg Gunner on by running full bore straight for Gunner's face. The second Gunner would make a move toward old Bradley, that darn cat would jump straight up into the air as Gunner would run under him, always giving Bradley the lead until Gunner stopped and turned around. Gunner loved to chase Bradley, which we could never really understand, as Gunner could never catch him. Even Penny and Panda would sit watching with amusement as Gunner and Bradley would cruise by them. One could almost hear the two beagle girls snickering, as if placing kibble bets on Bradley the cat as the winner.

Of course, that was not the only New England snickering that was aimed at Gunner and me. Let's face it, both Gunner and I were the classic "fish out of water" story from the moment we arrived in New England. Both of us were raised in the southwest. Oh, I was born in Pennsylvania, but I had moved to New Mexico at age four. At that early age, I don't think I had quite yet manifested my snow legs or an eastern flare. Gunner and I managed to survive the hotter-than-normal summer with its high humidity. Coming from the dry climate of a desert state, I was not used to such high humidity. It felt more like the jungles of Africa. To add to this, I asked Cathy on one particularly hot day if we could turn up the air conditioner.

Laughing, she said, "We don't have air conditioners in New England."

"Okay, and why is that?" I asked.

She explained that it usually never gets very hot in New England. In fact, every New Englander I came in contact with told me they never had heat like this before in these parts. Sure, I thought to myself, and then I did what any red-blooded southwesterner would do. I ran out to Sears and purchased not one, but three window air conditioners for Cathy's two-story home. I was convinced that this was basic survival for Gunner and me. Cathy humored me by allowing me to install the air conditioners throughout the house and never said a word. Once I was done with my project, I was rather pleased with myself and with the cooler air now circulating throughout Cathy's house. While Cathy would never admit to it, which I would assume is some unwritten oath New Englanders take at an early age, I think she liked it, too.

My next encounter with New England involved basic speech problems. I went out into the backyard one day. I found Cathy talking to her next-door neighbor, John.

"You got your shots on," John said, looking at me with a big smile on his face.

"Shots?" I repeated with a dumfounded look on

my face. I then did what any red blooded American male would do. I looked down to make sure my zipper was up. I was trying to figure out what in the world "shots" were and how I put them on when I did not know what they were.

"Your shots," John repeated, still smiling.

Thank God Cathy was there. She explained later that evening that New Englanders pronounce their R's as A's and their A's as R's. While it took me another minute to digest this, I finally realized my "shots" were my cargo shorts. Once I got that down pat, I figured I was good-to-go, right? Wrong! When Cathy and I would go out to dinner and I would order from the menu, many times the waitresses would ask where I was from. I would simply reply, "New Mexico."

"My, you speak such good English for being from Mexico."

I learned after the first time to just nod, as many just could not wrap their brain around the difference between New Mexico and Mexico. God forbid I should utter the words "you all." For when I did, heads would turn and look at me like I was from another planet.

While I was dealing with the language issues, poor Gunner became mail-delivery challenged there in New England. No, it wasn't that he wasn't getting his copy of American Beagle or anything simple like that. This was by far a more physical issue. At home, Gunner and I lived in the country, where rural mailboxes were where they should be—out at the end of your driveway. Here in Norwood, however, mail was delivered via a slot in the front door. The mailman would open the slot and drop the mail into the house. Penny and Panda grew up with this mail delivery system and were accustomed to it. In fact, Cathy said one of the postal workers would sometimes drop Milk Bones through the slot for the girls. However, by the time Gunner got to Norwood, with its strange, new postal delivery system, all that came through the mail slot was mail.

This was fine, until one day when I was eating lunch in the kitchen and the slot opened. Gunner ran to the door to watch what I assume he thought was a possessed mail slot that tossed mail in at him. To his and my surprise, in came a large—we are talking huge, possibly mega-size, or at least three-ton—magazine that hit him in the head. From that moment on, Gunner had it in for the postman. Every time he would drop mail through the slot, Gunner barked at him and

13

would run to each window in the house in order to see the mailman make his way past Cathy's house. It was Gunner's responsibility to protect the complete family and chase this evil mail-toting man away.

After summer came a beautiful autumn, which covered the ground with an amazing carpet of golden leaves from the two giant maple trees in Cathy's backyard. Not to mention the one in the neighbor's front yard. I thought it looked absolutely beautiful, that is, until I had to rake all those leaves up. Here again, I was not prepared for what was to follow. In New England, when fall arrives and the leaves begin to fall, they fall and fall and fall. I am sure there were at least four bazillion tons of leaves in Cathy's yard alone. I tried to do what we southwesterners do in fall, which is to rake and bag the leaves. Soon I was knee deep in those stupid golden leaves. Cathy noticed the leaves were gaining momentum on me and told me she kept an old flat bed sheet in the shed. I must have had a total look of confusion on my face, so she explained that I was to simply rake the leaves onto the large bed sheet. From there I was to get the large bags from the shed and fill them using huge leaf tongs. I had wondered what those things were for; they resembled a huge pair of salad tongs. Who knows, maybe these people in New England were just really into their salads in a big way, or at least when serving it up. However, fallen leaves were not the only thing I was not prepared for.

I flew home to get some of my winter clothes in September. When I arrived back in New England, Cathy watched me unpack.

She asked, "Where is your winter coat?"

I quickly picked up what I wore out in New Mexico in the winter, and she asked once again.

"Okay, now where is your winter coat?"

Obviously she did not understand what I was saying to her and we must have had some type of communication issue there, or she hated my coat. However, it was I who failed to understand and found myself getting a Coat 101 lesson from Cathy. Did you know they even have a rating system that pertains to the temperatures these parkas are rated for? Well, they do; and within a week, Cathy had a brand new parka for me with a four-snowflake rating.

"Try it on," she said as she held it out to me.

As I tried on the parka, a memory of my childhood came rushing back to me. I think every kid has this same memory: you know, the one where your mom bundles you up on a winter day and you look like the cousin to the Michelin Man. Then she opens the front door and tells you to have fun playing. However, you can barely even move enough to make your way toward the door, let alone play in the darn coat.

At any rate, winter followed; and my first big snow while staying in New England was, to me, mesmerizing, to say the least. I loved it. In fact, this was my first experience with a snow shovel and Gus, the snowplow guy. When the snow first began to fall, I was upstairs in the bedroom that Cathy and I converted to an office for me, so I could do my article writing and website design. I quickly saved my work on the computer and ran downstairs to get the snow shovel. I think somewhere east of the Mississippi God has a rule about snow that I did not remember from my four short years in Pennsylvania as a child. I say this because two things kept happening that I, being from the southwest, was totally clueless about. First, each time I cleared Cathy's driveway, Gus the snowplow guy miraculously appeared out of nowhere and began clearing the street out front, which, I might add, put approximately three to four feet of snow at the front of her driveway. So while I was busy clearing the snow from Gus the snowplow guy, God was busy dumping more snow in Cathy's driveway right behind me. After a few hours of God and Gus the snowplow guy having their fun with me, I returned to the house while Gunner, Penny, and Panda watched me from the window by the stairs. It was Gunner whose face seemed to beam with pride, as if his beagle dad had pioneered and forged a path for all the family to venture out. However, both Penny and Panda, being New England beagles, knew Gus and God were winning and I was beat.

That same storm laid foot after foot of snow all over New England, but I think most of it fell in Cathy's yard, in particular, her backyard, where I had to clear a path for the beagles, so they could go outside. One morning, while I cleared Cathy's deck as best as I could, I began navigating the stairs off the deck going down into the yard. It was then that I think I broke all downhill skiing records, at least for deck stair skiing, that is. Gunner stood back looking like I had just accomplished the most miraculous stunt on this earth. If he could have applauded with pride, he would have. Penny and Panda, on the other hand (or paw), cleared away as if one of the large maple trees was falling instead of me. You see, while Gunner was clueless about what was happening, Penny and Panda knew a snow klutz when they saw one.

I think I heard the beagles snicker once more that morning, but it wasn't quite as loud as the laughter coming from inside the house, from Cathy. It finally dawned on me that New Englanders import guys like Gunner and me just for the entertainment value. After all, those long cold winters can get pretty boring.

Our first Christmas together followed, and to me it was amazing. Everything looked like a page right out of a Norman Rockwell painting. As a bachelor, I simply did not celebrate Christmas. It just did not make any sense for me to put up a tree and decorate when I traveled so much and lived alone. But now here we were, the five of us spending the holidays together. The season took on a completely new meaning for me after that. However, it did not go without some excitement. After Cathy meticulously decorated our tree (and I do mean meticulously), I watched as Penny went right behind Cathy to add her touch, or paw, to the decorations around the house. Penny loved to lie under the Christmas tree, which was not an issue until it was time for her to get up. It was the getting up part that broke several decorations and removed strands of lights each day. It was not uncommon to see Penny walking as if nothing was wrong with a trail of Christmas lights following her into the next room. Needless to say, it was all part of a great experience for me.

As spring neared, Cathy and I traveled back to New Mexico to put my house on the market. After we met with my realtor to determine when to sell, Cathy said those few words every realtor loves to hear, "So, how much do houses go for in this area?" The next thing I remember was seeing nothing but taillights and a cloud of dust as Cathy and Irma, the realtor, hit the road in search of houses. Nah, I figured it was just a passing phase. After all, Cathy had lived, been educated, and had worked in the east all her life.

After her jaunt around Albuquerque with Irma, we were flying back to Norwood, back to our beagles, Gunner, Penny, and Panda, and back to the snow. Somewhere at about 30,000 feet on a jet bound for Logan International Airport,

Cathy turned to me and said, "I'm going home to put my house on the market."

"Oxygen, aisle 10, window seat." No, not for me. I figured *she* must be short of oxygen, why else would she be saying such foolishness? Once again, I thought that after we got our feet on the ground she would forget this silly notion. I said nothing more on the subject to her; that is, until Joe, her realtor, came to the house the very next Monday. You see, Cathy was a woman with a plan. She figured we needed an "our" house! Not *his* house or *her* house but one we could call our own and create new memories in, our memories. Okay, I guess this made sense. We decided to keep my house so we would have a place to live until we found our home. Thirty days later, Cathy's home sold.

Bound for New Mexico

WHILE GUNNER WAS crate trained, Penny and Panda were not. In fact, I think it is safe to say they both hated crates. It did not matter what it looked like or what was in it. I believe the two girls had a theory: if it looked like a crate and smelled like a crate, by golly it was a crate, and they wanted nothing to do with it. Cathy and I tried to feed them in it for weeks to get them ready for air travel. During that time, Penny and Panda learned to stretch their necks to the greatest length possible to eat their meals, yet they never had to place a single foot into the crate. Shoot, I even climbed in the thing to show them it was okay. They both looked at me like I was nuts, and all my efforts did nothing, except make my back and neck hurt.

At the end of April, the snow was still falling in Norwood. We packed everything we could and watched the movers load it onto a moving van headed for New Mexico. Cathy and I packed up the three beagles and whatever the truck did not haul away. We attached a large sign with each beagle's name and a final destination to each of the crates. The night before we said goodbye to New England we stayed in a pet-friendly hotel in Rhode Island, close to the airport.

The next morning, we made it to the airport with the beagles in tow. Once there, we were greeted with at least a ream of paper to fill out for the beagles in order to transport them. After what seemed like forever in people years, forget about dog years, the beagles were loaded onto the plane, which had a layover in Houston, Texas. We worried ourselves sick with the "what ifs." When the flight was called and we boarded the plane, we asked one of the flight attendants if she could please check to make sure our three beagles were onboard. The airline held the flight up while they radioed to make sure Gunner, Penny, and Panda were safely onboard and not out for a bowl of kibble in the airport lobby.

Needless to say, we received a few nasty looks from the other passengers. However, in a few minutes we got the thumbs up from the front of the cabin and off we went.

Upon arrival in Albuquerque, Cathy and I were totally jetlagged but happy for all five of us to be home together. Well, at least we thought we were all together. Cathy and I waited and waited in the designated area where the beagles were to be brought to us. Let's face it, the designated area was nothing fancy, nor was it really secure. It was simply the baggage claim area. Nervously, Cathy wandered off. Suddenly, I turned to see a frantic Cathy running in my direction.

"Panda just came out on a conveyer belt thing," she said, out of breath.

While I was still attempting to make sense of why Panda was being delivered to us on a baggage conveyer belt, where anyone could have taken her if they wanted to, Cathy was worried sick as to Gunner and Penny's whereabouts. Okay, we had a full-blown beagle emergency on our hands. We only had one of three beagles; not good odds and certainly not the way we wanted our new lives to begin here in New Mexico.

There was no stopping Cathy at this point. Like General George Patton firing orders at the troops, I was told to get Panda. She headed off for security before I could salute or blink. Gunner and Penny, even with the large signs taped on each of their crates with their names and final destination, Albuquerque, New Mexico in large block letters, were somehow on the flight getting ready to depart for Cancun, Mexico. Cathy informed me that security was trying to stop the aircraft so that they could unload the two beagle stowaways.

I thought to myself that Gunner and Penny must have conned the baggage handlers into letting them have a much-needed beagle vacation without Panda or us. You know, a romantic little beagle get-away just for the two of them. Shoot, it was almost like the two lovers on the Titanic. One could almost hear Céline Dion singing the theme song from the soundtrack of *Titanic* in the background and see Penny's beautiful, long beagle ears flowing in the breeze as Gunner held onto her like Leonardo DiCaprio holding Kate Winslet. Okay, so that was a little over the top. Needless to say, we still had two beagles missing.

While I tried to calm Cathy down and remain

calm myself, we waited for what seemed like an hour until Gunner and Penny came out, escorted by security, their little get-away plan foiled by Panda and Cathy. Gunner and Penny looked quite innocent...as if to say, would we do that?

After we collected our two stowaways and the rest of our belongings, we headed off to my home, just outside of Albuquerque. Penny realized New Mexico was to her liking. She loved the New Mexico sunshine. In fact, one could say Penny was a sun worshiper. Like Trixie in the *Hi and Lois* comic strips, Penny loved her sunbeam and looked forward to it each day. She would lay out in the yard on her back with all four legs up in the air. When you took a closer look, you could see her eyes wide open, as if she were daydreaming while she looked up into the clear blue sky. On the other paw, as they say, Panda was like a New England snowman ready to melt into a puddle on the front deck. She hated the heat. I am sure if she could have mastered the phone, she would have booked herself on the first flight back to New England.

It was shortly after our return to New Mexico that I decided to ask Cathy to marry me. I went to a jewelry store and looked at engagement rings. Nothing had the look I wanted. When I was getting ready to leave, I turned to my left and there it was—a beautiful engagement ring. I asked the clerk if I could see the ring. Not only did she pull the ring from the locked glass case, but she also grabbed me and pulled me through the mall until we were outside in the sunlight.

"Look how beautifully the diamonds catch the light," she said, holding her hand upward.

"Uh-huh," I said, nodding my head, still in shock from being pulled through a mall by a sales clerk.

"Is this the one?" she asked.

"Well…ah, can I afford it?"

We went back inside, and after hearing the price, I realized it was much more than I could afford. However, each time I looked at that ring, I knew it was the one I wanted for Cathy—if she would marry me. I decided I would put the ring on layaway and move forward.

Oh my God, I thought to myself, *I am really going to ask her*. For two weeks I thought about and planned the right way to ask her.

On April 25, Cathy planned to go to lunch and do some shopping. At lunch, the waiter came out with a long stemmed red rose and presented it along with a note. From the note, Cathy had to decipher where the next clue could be found. Off Cathy went in search of the next clue. At each stop, Cathy found another rose, and yet another clue.

Finally, she found a bottle floating in a fountain with a message inside. This last clue took her to a hotel, where the clerk handed her the key to a suite. When Cathy opened the door to the suite, she found that I had placed rose petals all over the carpet and bed. I had a big white teddy bear sitting on the table with a note asking her to go down to the lobby at 4:00 p.m. She would receive her next clue then. At 4:00, Cathy was in the lobby when a man called out her name and gave her twelve long stem white roses and asked her to come with him. Cathy stepped outside and was escorted to a limo, where I was waiting. Thinking I was taking her to a romantic dinner, she got in. The limo driver had prior orders to take us to the top of the Sandia Mountains. We stopped just shy of the top, and he opened our door. We walked down a pathway until we got to a large rock. I asked Cathy to stop and sit down. It was there that I gave her the last note. As she was reading it, I got down on one knee.

"I would be honored if you would marry me. But if you need time to think about it, I understand," I said, looking up at her.

"Yes, Tim."

"Really? I understand if you need time."

"Tim, I said yes. I want to marry you."

We were now officially engaged. Only then did I pull the ring out from my pocket and place it on her hand. She loved it.

Penny and Panda

WITH CATHY AND I now officially engaged, the bond between Penny and I grew stronger each day, and Cathy and Gunner became increasingly closer. Gradually, Panda began to realize she could depend on me as well. The process, however, took baby steps at first. I began to notice a change in our relationship when Panda injured her front paw. She had been digging around a large bush and had managed to cut her pad. After arriving at the vet's office, Cathy took her into the exam room as I waited in the lobby for them. When the exam door opened up, Panda pulled loose from Cathy's grip and limped as fast as she could across the lobby floor in her bright purple bandage, never stopping until she cuddled up next to me. With a surprised expression on my face, I looked up at Cathy in amazement and shock. It was then that both Cathy and I realized Panda, too, was finally becoming a daddy's little girl.

Since Penny and Panda had the same biological parents, and were separated by a mere litter, it was a challenge for many people to tell them apart, myself included. Cathy had to point out on more than one occasion that Penny had less white in her tail than Panda did. This helped me sometimes, until I saw that Penny and Panda would lay down with their tails tucked neatly underneath them. So without the "tell-tale tail," I found that I was still at a loss.

Nonetheless, I think looks are where the genetic roadmap stopped for Penny and Panda. It was easy to see that their personalities and traits were not the same. Panda's personality was very serious, hard to be pleased. She was very cautious and slow to bond with humans or other animals. However, once she did, her loyalty to that human or other pet was extremely deep and devoted. The contrast between the two girls was also evident at playtime. Penny loved to run and play with squeaky toys and would do so for long periods of time. In our household, it was not uncommon to hear Penny running through the house with a squeaky toy dangling from her mouth squeaking as Gunner chased after her doing the same. However, Panda was our observer, as she would sit back and watch Penny and Gunner play. Squeaky toys were of no interest to her.

One thing was very apparent: Panda loved Penny and Penny was extremely protective of Panda. Whether animals are capable of understanding that they came from the same set of parents is truly a mystery I think. However, Panda and Penny knew there was a connection between them.

Penny's persona was extremely independent. The fact is, if Penny would have had two legs rather than four, I would go so far as to say she would have been a highly successful female entrepreneur. A classic example of this is a time when I had taken ill, was laid up in bed, and could not walk the beagles. When Cathy walked the beagles by herself, she would always take two and then come back for the third one. While this worked the first day, Penny decided she was quite capable of walking herself. Cathy hooked up both Panda and Gunner to their leashes and opened our front door. Before she knew it, Penny trotted out the front door with a matter-of-fact look upon her face. There stood Cathy, attached to Panda and Gunner, and unable to really go after Penny. Penny looked at her as if to say, so what's the problem here? I have it all under control.

Cathy first turned back toward our front door, assuming Penny would follow. However, that was not going to happen, not in Penny's mind at least. Not until she had her daily walk. Cathy then proceeded to take the path we always walked the beagles on. Several steps in front of Cathy and the other beagles was Penny, leading the way. Not once did she stray from them during their walk. As they completed the walk and circled back to our house, Cathy unlocked our front door. In walked Penny, with the expression of complete contentment written all over her face.

Prairie Dogs, Jaws, and Thunderstorms

*P*ENNY FOUND THAT THE country way of life fit her perfectly. There was just so much in the form of smells and creatures that she was never bored for a second. Each day in New Mexico was an adventure for her. Her first newfound friends were a colony of prairie dogs that lived behind the Chevron station a few miles from my home. Cathy and I were driving home with the three beagles in the backseat of the car when Penny's keen eye spotted her very first prairie dog. We dubbed him Prairie Dog Pete. As if he knew Penny was watching him as we turned the corner, Prairie Dog Pete stood there in the middle of the street on his hind legs. I stopped to let the little prairie dog cross the road. Penny stood with her two front paws up on the console between Cathy and me and watched Prairie Dog Pete with the amazement of a child at Christmastime. From that moment on, Penny loved prairie dogs.

In fact, on one of our outings, I found a postcard of a prairie dog and purchased it for Penny. I made a frame for it out of pine in my woodworking shop. I painted the wood Penny's signature color, which was pink. After the pink paint dried, I hand painted white dog bones on the frame and put it in Penny and Panda's room. Oh yes, Penny and Panda had their very own bedroom. Like so many couples with pets as surrogate children, our beagles had their own space. If you had walked into our home and not known better, you would have looked at the room and thought it was a little girl's room— which was true, just two little beagle girls with just a little more hair and two extra legs.

At any rate, the country seemed to bring out a part of Penny's personality that had not been evident in New England. Like so many pets, Penny had her share of nicknames. Her first one here in New Mexico was Ellie Mae, after the character on *The Beverly Hillbillies*. Much like Ellie

Mae, Penny was a friend to all creatures large and small. Penny became one with the vast lands of New Mexico.

The one thing Penny hated without a shadow of a doubt, whether we lived on the East or West Coast, was the vacuum cleaner, which we nicknamed Jaws. When Jaws came out to do his work, Penny would have preferred to not live in the same ZIP code, or even the same area code for that matter. It was then, in hindsight, that I guess Cathy and I should have noticed a pattern forming with Penny and loud noises; they were upsetting to her. The fact is, she didn't even like her tags clanking against her food bowl, so Cathy got a little pocket-like device for her collar. Cathy was able to tuck the tags inside of it, so there would be no more tag noise to upset her. However, both of us assumed that the vacuum just hurt Penny's ears. Penny would always go outside until Jaws was put away. When she knew that darn vacuum cleaner was gone, only then would she enter the house.

Another issue that surfaced in New Mexico that was not as prevalent while living in New England was her fear of thunderstorms. While I would never go so far as to tell anyone thunderstorms do not exist in New England, what I will say is New Mexico can have a perfectly calm, picture-perfect blue sky one minute, and the next, a raging thunderstorm with lightning streaking all across the desert sky. This can be a daily event during certain months of the year. We were never really sure why Penny feared lightning and thunderstorms out here so much, but we noticed her fear worsened each year. Penny could sense an oncoming storm long before it ever got here. We could always tell that a thunderstorm was heading our way when Penny disappeared into our bedroom.

With me working out of a home office, I could act quickly when I noticed a change in Penny's behavior. I attempted to do everything humanly possible to ease the stress of an approaching storm. My actions resembled that of a man battening down the hatches in preparation for a storm. In reality, I was transforming our bedroom into "the cave," Penny's haven during a thunderstorm. I would quickly go downstairs and close the blinds in our bedroom. I reasoned with myself that this would lessen the chance of her seeing the flash from the lightning. Next, I turned the bedside lamp on. Again, my theory behind this was simple. As the clouds rolled across the New Mexico desert sky, our bedroom became darker than normal; added to this equation was the fact that the blinds were closed. When the lightning rolled like a powerful ball of electricity across the sky, it created flashes of light in the darkened room. Therefore, the bedside lamp provided a stable light source and the room did not light up each time the lightning illuminated the sky outside. Next, I would turn on the television, figuring the noise would help to drown out the thunder that roared from above.

This worked somewhat, until one day Penny left her thunderstorm hideaway beneath our bed and came upstairs into my office, shaking from her head to her beagle toes. When I convinced her to come back downstairs with me, I found out why she left her refuge. Cathy had been watching The Weather Channel the day before, so there on the screen of our television set was an episode of "Storm Stories," with a raging thunderstorm piping in the very noise I was attempting to drown out. From that day on, Penny joined the ranks of devoted QVC frequent shoppers whenever a storm darkened our beautiful blue New Mexico skies. Along with closing the blinds and turning on the bedside lamp, I turned on the shopping channel. From beneath our bed, Penny could wait out the storm and shop to her heart's content.

Her favorite segment on QVC was the jewelry section, which was no surprise to Cathy or me. Each time Cathy took off her engagement ring to wash her hands or put on lotion, Penny would stand on her hind legs trying to get those jewels. We never quite understood Penny's attraction to diamonds and jewelry; nonetheless, she could smell a diamond a mile away and further proved the theory that a diamond was a beagle girl's best friend.

Several months later, while researching an upcoming article I was doing for *OurDogHouse.com* about thunderstorms and pets, I ran across a unique product that was said to aid pets in stressful situations such as thunderstorms. It was a wrap designed to use maintained pressure. In theory, maintained pressure helps to calm the sensory receptors that report to the brain, resulting in a calmer dog. I quickly researched everything I could find on the wrap and then purchased one. We knew all too well that until it was Penny-approved, all the research in the world meant nothing to us. The literature recommended putting the wrap on the pet at different times so the pet would not associate the wrap solely with storms or other stressful events. So that is what we did. We called it her Super Beagle outfit.

When the first true test presented itself in the form of a storm, I had Penny dressed in her Super Beagle outfit; and it really did seem to take the edge off the storm for her. Gunner and Panda did not know what to make of her in her new outfit, but I assume they just figured it was one of the items Penny found she could not live without on QVC.

While Penny was attempting to adjust to the thunderstorms here in the southwest, Cathy and I were looking for that perfect *our* home.

The Our House

WITH IRMA, THE realtor, guiding us through listing after listing, Cathy and I created a wish list for what we wanted in a home. We quickly found out that her wants and wishes and his wants and wishes did not exist in the same house—at least not here in New Mexico, and not in our price range. Each property we looked at had either the perfect backyard any beagle would gladly put his or her paw of approval on, or the right house, but not both. There was always a "but" in the way. No, not that kind of butt, rather…but it lacked a kitchen Cathy liked,…but the dining room was too small, or…but the garage would not accommodate my woodworking tools—a struggle I am sure most couples go through. I began to wonder how Cathy and I could possibly want such different things. It seemed like we were on opposite ends of the spectrum in what we each wanted in a house. At times, I found myself focusing on this rather than the house Irma was showing.

However, the one thing we knew we needed was a nice yard for our beagles to play in. We needed to come back to the basic foundation of our relationship, which was our love for each other, along with our love and devotion to our beagles. On the last search for an *our* house, I pulled Irma aside and told her I would back away from my wish list and I wanted her to just find us a house that Cathy liked and the beagles could be happy with. That afternoon Irma brought us back to the very first house she had shown us when we started looking. We looked at it again and made an offer. We moved in the following week.

The new home was just inside the Albuquerque city limits. Both Penny and I had some adjustment issues to manage, which were not easy for either one of us. I was raised in the country and loved the open space, and so did Penny. At the same time, I was busy fixing up my old home with the intention of putting it on the market. I like to refer to this period as Penny's and my weaning period from the country.

I always took the beagles with me when I went to my house to work, mainly because I wanted Penny to be able to roam and play in the large yard. She was more than content to sniff the property over and look for critters for hours. Then, as the afternoon sunshine presented itself from above, Penny would find that perfect spot to lie in upside down and daydream. As with all good things, this had to come to an end. I was working in my office in the new house when Irma called and presented me with an offer on my home. I accepted it.

Shortly after the sale of my country home, Penny gained her next nickname. We called her Gretchen, after the popular country western singer, Gretchen Wilson, who is famous for the song "Redneck Woman." That was our Penny, only she was our Redneck Beagle Woman here in the big city; and like Gretchen's song, if Penny could have left her Christmas lights on the front porch of her dog house all year long, she would have. Gone was Prairie Dog Pete; gone was Penny's country home along with all the critters and smells of country living. When a critter ventured into our new neighborhood from time to time, Penny was the first one to know about it. Shoot, I think a big black grizzly bear could have tapped Gunner on the shoulders and asked for directions and he would not have noticed anything unusual. And Panda, of course, needed only an air conditioner and a comfy bed to make her happy. Nevertheless, after several months, we all settled into our home.

Here Comes the Beagle, I Mean, Bride

*I*T IS OFTEN SAID that every bride is beautiful on her wedding day. In our case, so was every beagle.

One year after our move from New England to New Mexico, Cathy decided our engagement had lasted long enough. It was time for her to set the date, which she did. She picked March 10, reasoning with me that this was a perfect date, since it was the day we first met face-to-face. Being a man, I looked at things from a logical perspective. I explained to Cathy that late spring or early fall was a much prettier time here in the southwest. March can run the gamut from wind that could turn your hairdo into a Phyllis Diller look-alike to downpours that could soak you to the bone.

While I was busy listing all the different months that were more weather-friendly, Cathy was busy planning our wedding for March 10. Finally, I came to my senses. Cathy did not need my input as to what the weather would be like in May or September. She had made up her mind. So I did what any smart man would do and asked her to let me know the details when she had them. Over the next few months, Cathy and I scouted out different locations, from churches to hotels, so she could decide where we would be married and where the reception would be. We wanted our beagles to be a part of our day in some way. After all, it was through our love of our beagles that we met.

Cathy did what every bride-to-be does, which is to go to at least four million bridal shops and try on at least six million dresses, looking into the mirror and shaking her head each time. Finally, after she had tried on every dress in the Albuquerque area at least once, and some twice, she picked the perfect dress for our wedding. In contrast, it took me about ten minutes for a tux fitting—in, out, and on my way. Next came the flowers, most of which I never knew even

45

existed. I knew this for certain when Cathy and the florist began talking about Queen Anne's lace going into her bridal bouquet. It took me several minutes to understand that this was not a piece of cloth, but rather a flower. I think it was around this time that I began working on what I like to refer to as the "nod of approval." This is a quality every husband-to-be needs to perfect before marriage.

Lastly, Cathy wanted to find something for the beagles to wear. Finding the items for Penny and Panda turned into a journey that was almost as long as finding the perfect wedding dress. Added to this dilemma was the fact that it had to match Cathy's dress—a rule, I am sure, only under-stood by a woman. Thus, being a male, I was clueless and unable to wrap my brain around the reason why Penny and Panda's outfit had to match her dress.

She searched the Internet and local shops and finally found two garters that matched perfectly. Oddly enough, Penny and Panda never seemed to mind wearing the garters (which are to be worn around a bride's leg) around their necks, and, frankly, they worked perfectly. Gunner wore a simple black bowtie around his neck. Finally, we had our four-legged wedding party outfitted for the occasion. Gunner looked stunning as the best beagle man. Penny and Panda were quite the picture in their lacy collars as the beagle maids of honor.

While Cathy was busy with wedding planning, I wanted to find a wedding gift for my bride-to-be. I went to the jewelry store where I had purchased her engagement ring and found, to my surprise, a necklace that matched her engagement ring perfectly. I purchased it on the spot. I left the necklace at the jewelry store until the night before our wedding. In my rush to get to the wedding rehearsal, I tossed the bag with the necklace in it under our bed so that Cathy would not find it. After the rehearsal and rehearsal dinner, a few family members accompanied us back to the house. Cathy went into the bedroom for a few minutes, leaving me and my future mother-in-law, JoAnne, in the great room. When her mother asked for her, I went into the bedroom and found Penny halfway under the bed.

"Funny, it's not storming," I said, looking over at Cathy pointing toward Penny's butt sticking out from under the bed skirt.

It was then I remembered the necklace I had purchased for Cathy to wear on our wedding day. I knew it was approximately in the same location under the bed where Penny was. Thinking back to all those times Penny would try to take Cathy's engagement ring, I quickly flopped to my knees and then onto my belly, trying to get under our bed. I am sure Cathy thought the stress of the upcoming nuptials had finally gotten to me, and I was possibly seeking refuge under our bed. I managed to lodge my entire upper torso under the bed with my butt and legs thrashing around outside. I was in the midst of war! A tug-of-war, that is, with Penny over the diamond necklace.

Penny, of course, had the home court advantage. She knew the underside of our bed much better than I. Plus, her beagle physique fit much better than that of a full-grown man. Once I was under the bed, Penny locked her jaws around the bag, refusing to give it up. She reminded me of a lady I once saw as a kid when there was a sale at a local store and another woman tried to take the item she wanted from the sales display. Most professional wrestlers could have taken lessons from these two ladies. Shoot, I think Penny figured QVC finally got around to sending one of the orders she had placed during the last storm and she was not going to give up the goods without a fight. Meanwhile, I might add, Cathy was seeing only half of what was going on—the bottom halves of both Penny and me sticking out from under the bed with my half still thrashing around. Cathy burst into uncontrollable laughter, which brought JoAnne rushing in to see what all the commotion was about. I'm sure it is moments such as these that cause every mother of the bride to wonder just what in the world her daughter could have ever seen in her future husband, and why the daughter did not have the good sense God gave her to say no when the man asked for her hand in marriage.

Cathy kept asking if I needed help, to which I kept replying, "no, dear, I could handle it." Perhaps Penny had a nose for diamonds, or maybe Gunner had let her in on a little secret and told her that those pretty lacy wedding collars were really garters that are to be worn on a leg and not the neck. Nonetheless, after several minutes, and a few bangs on the head—mine that is—it was Cathy who wore her brand-new diamond necklace as she and her father Frank walked down the aisle and the pianist played Pachelbel's Canon on our wedding day. Penny and Panda wore their lacy garters, and Gunner had his stunning black bowtie on. In reflecting back, Cathy, Penny, and Panda were beautiful, and Gunner was very handsome on our special day; and I would not have changed a thing, not even that Queen Ann's Lace stuff that should be a piece of cloth, not a flower.

Beagle Partners in Crime

WITH ONE HOUSE, A NEW marriage and the three beagles, we all began to settle into a routine. Well, one would think that was what was to happen; and, for the most part, it did. Cathy went to work in the Human Resources department for a company with headquarters based here in the Albuquerque area. I went back to school part-time at the University of New Mexico and enrolled in a master's program in website design.

Outside the house in my spare time, I began the construction of flowerbeds that lined the complete back walls of our backyard. While I was at it, I decided to add a bubbler system to water the plant life as well. I managed to turn our backyard into a full-blown beagle hardhat area with trenches in the ground and tools and long PVC pipe piled everywhere.

I once overheard a guy in a home improvement store tell his wife, "Men build 'cause they can't give birth." While I have never wanted to give birth, nor have I known any male friends that would want to, I would agree for the most part that us guys like to build things.

The beagles, especially Penny, loved it when I worked in the backyard. Penny's face always expressed her inquisitive nature. Each item I brought into the backyard had to go through her thorough inspection. However, there was an added bonus for all three of them while I was changing the face of the landscape. As I dug the trenches, dirt they had not been able to sniff before surfaced, requiring extra beagle inspections.

Shortly after the completion of the flowerbeds, installation of the bubbler system, and the addition of new plant life, Panda took up a hobby: horticulture. As Panda became one with nature, the gardening side of her personality came out in full bloom. We could find Panda nestled beneath a rose bush or surrounded by dozens of colorful daisies. The variety of flower did not matter to Panda; she loved all the flowers. In fact, I truly believe that, in her mind, I had done all this for her, not Cathy. It wasn't until she began to resemble a John Deere backhoe with her digging habits in the flowerbeds that it became an issue. No matter what we did, we could not keep her from her flowers. While we really did not mind her sleeping amongst the roses, daisies, and verbena, her digging presented a challenge for the plants themselves.

After many failed attempts to train her not to get into the flowerbeds, we purchased a small decorative garden fence to line the flowerbeds and restrict beagle access, which served only to keep the other two beagles out and not Panda. So while Panda laid in her bed of roses, Penny found something equally entertaining to keep herself busy in the summer months.

When we moved in, the previous owners had an area in the backyard equipped for a swing set for their small children. When they moved out, they took the swing set with them, leaving behind a large area covered in deep white sand that seemed to call Penny's name each time she exited our back door. After all, Penny loved her sunshine; she now discovered she had the added benefit of a sandy beach to go along with it. Really, all that was missing for her was an ice cold bowl of water with a tiny little umbrella sticking out of it. She could close her eyes and almost feel like she was basking on a warm beach in Cancun. So, on any given day in the summertime, our backyard resembled an all-inclusive beagle vacation hideaway. Panda was busy networking with the flowerbeds. Gunner could be found kicked back on one of our patio chairs on the porch, looking like he was contemplating his 401(k)-9 account or some other matter that required deep thought. Penny was at her beach, beagle tanning. The lush green grass that grew, I can only assume, was for me to mow and water, as it did not seem to be of any attraction to the beagles.

Penny's beach-going habits did not seem to be a problem at first. However, as the summer wore on and Penny went to the beach every chance she got, she resembled Pig Pen in the Peanuts cartoon with a plume of dirt and dust following her everywhere she went, including our house. The three beagles went for regular grooming sessions; nonetheless, that would not last for long. In fact, I had the timing down to a science: Penny would get out of my truck in the garage, walk into the house, and head for the backdoor. Within seconds of getting home from her bath and the beagle day spa, she was upside down at her beach in the sand.

Cathy figured if she went outside with Penny, it would put a halt to the sand play for Penny. Not hardly! In concept, it seemed workable to Cathy. Nevertheless, Penny knew enough to wait until something attracted Cathy's attention from her—the "something" being none other than her sister, Panda. Somehow Penny and Panda had a strategy worked out between them. Like many small children I have seen in the past, even without words, they seem to be able to communicate in ways we just cannot fathom. Panda would make her way into the flowerbeds, taking Cathy's attention away from Penny just long enough for Penny to roll around on her sunny beach, stopping only long enough to lie on her back and gaze up into the blue picturesque New Mexico sky.

Penny's beautiful, shiny coat would go from the lustrous shine she came home with to a dull coat of sand, dust, and grit. Cathy reminded me of a mother who had just dressed her daughter up in a frilly party dress only to have the little girl climbing trees and playing in the dirt and mud. Oddly, it seemed the more upset Cathy got and the harder she would try to get Penny to stop playing in the sand, the more Penny enjoyed rolling in it. Or maybe she just liked the red in Cathy's face; I was really never sure. It was times such as these that I did everything I could to not laugh at them.

I realized that to preserve sanity within the household, I needed to do something with the sand patch. So while Cathy was away on a business trip, the three beagles and I picked out some beautiful flagstone and had it installed. This created a beautiful patio in the garden that was surrounded by our roses. Penny was not thrilled with the idea; however, in time she found the lush green grass to her liking for her sunbathing purposes. After the beagles and I constructed the flowerbeds in the backyard, we had more work cut out for us.

Each time I found a new project around the house to take on, the beagles, Penny in particular, greeted it with childlike curiosity. Another dog owner once told me that a dog loves you unconditionally: they will never pass judgment, will always listen to you, and will never tell you that you look fat. Added to that list should also be that a dog believes you can always accomplish what you set out to do. Project after project, my three helpers were right there by my side. Only a few times did they let me down. Like the time my sister-in-law, Karen, was coming to visit, and I decided I would help by washing all the windows inside and out. In theory, how hard could this be?

It wasn't until I got to the guest room upstairs that I realized there could be a problem. I washed the inside of the guest room window. As I was finishing up I noticed there was no place to put my ladder to wash the outside. However, if I slid the window open, I could simply step out onto the garage rooftop. I gathered up all the rags and window cleaner I needed, and then opened the window. I stepped out, shutting the window behind me. Penny, Panda, and Gunner watched me wash the window from the other side of the glass. It wasn't until after I finished cleaning the window that I realized I could not open the window from the outside. There I was with the sun rising over our house and the New Mexico temperature climbing at a rapid rate. Sweat rolled off me slowly at first; however, after a few minutes in the increasing heat, I was soaked. I gave up on the thought of not getting handprints on the clean window. Forget that! I placed the palms of both hands on the glass and began pressing and pulling to one side. The window did not budge. As I looked inside at the three beagles, I realized I must be quite entertaining to them. For the first time in my life, I was on the outside with no means to let myself in. I am sure they could fully relate to my pawing at the glass.

Since Cathy was at work, I figured it would be late afternoon before she would realize something was up, like her husband was stuck on the rooftop like Santa Claus when Rudolph and the eight tiny reindeer made off with the sleigh without him. While the beagles seemed amused by my dilemma, my beagle partners in crime just stood on the other side of the glass, watching me pawing the window to get in. Even when I tried bribing them by offering treats if they would just get help like Lassie would have in the movies, all I got was tail wags. While I was glad to offer the beagles some great entertainment, the New Mexico heat was becoming unbearable. After walking to the side of the roof, I calculated the drop and how much damage that would do to an already inoperable back. Deciding that was not an option, I walked back to the window and pawed as hard as I could on the glass. Finally, I was able to budge the window a few inches. Once I had enough room to stick my fingertips through, I slid the window open.

"Some help you guys are!" I said.

With sweat dripping off me, I climbed through the window. It was a relief to be back inside the air-conditioned house. The three beagles wagged their tails in beagle applause for my performance.

With company coming, it was only fitting that we take the beagles to be groomed. We had recently purchased our first vehicle with electric windows. Cathy and I loaded the three beagles in the backseat of the Toyota and off we went. I remember hearing a noise and feeling a whoosh of air on the back of my neck. Turning around, I discovered two beagle butts in my view. The rest of the beagle bodies were hanging out the back window. Gunner and Panda had managed to master the electric windows within the first couple of miles, even without opposable thumbs, and had decided they would take a detour. After all, it was only Aunt Karen coming to visit, and she had a dog, so she knew what dogs smelled like anyway.

"Cathy," I said as calmly as I could, "please turn around and GRAB PANDA AND GUNNER!"

Cathy, reading my expression, quickly turned and was able to grab them while I tried to put the window up. As quickly as I would get the darn window up, they would press the button and down went the window again. It took me a few minutes to find the child-proof locks or, in this case, beagle-proof locks for the windows and door in order to stop the Beagle partners in crime.

Penny 10 weeks old

ny 3 months old

Penny 10 moths old

Panda and Penny

Penny and Panda

Penny
Christmas 1

Penny and Gunner

*Penny, Panda,
and Gunner*

*Halloween
Panda, Gunner
and Penny*

Penny

Penny

Penny, Tyler, and Panda
© Kim Jew photography

Every Beagle Has a Season

*T*HEY SAY EVERYTHING has a season, like when spring gives way to the long days of summer and summer relinquishes her warm days to fall. People and pets have their seasons, too.

As the days turned into years, Cathy and I felt like the beagles had become our surrogate children. We had adopted them, or they adopted us, and they were simply an extension of our family. They celebrated holidays with us, and they each had their unique personalities. We loved them all dearly. Nonetheless, nothing lasts forever. Gunner was aging, and his health was beginning to fail.

Cathy and I took him to five different vets, desperately praying for a much needed miracle.

After x-rays and blood tests, we were told there was nothing that could be done, but no one could really tell us what it was we were fighting. We only knew Gunner would be fine for a while, and then he would have long bouts when he could not eat and would need to be on IV fluids to keep him going. Finally, the vet taught Cathy and I how to do the IV fluids at home to keep him hydrated, therefore allowing Gunner to be home rather than in the hospital. However, Gunner was in a lot of pain. As sick as he was, he knew when he got bad that I would take him to the vet. At times like these, he would walk over and stand by the garage door waiting for me to pack his favorite stuffed teddy bear, named Pooky Bear, and take them both to the vet.

Late on the night of January 1, he walked over to the garage door. Cathy called the vet and I packed up Gunner and Pooky Bear and drove over there. After the vet examined him again, she came out and sat to talk with me. She explained that she felt Gunner's time had come; his heart was racing, he wasn't able to eat on his own and he was in a lot of pain. That night, Gunner, at age 11 years and 3 months, made his last trip to the vet. He never returned home with me. I honestly have no idea how I managed to drive home through the tears.

I got home around 4:00 a.m. on the morning of January 3 after his passing. Cathy had left the stereo on in the living room the night before. I am not sure why but I walked over to the stereo and just stood there staring blankly through our front window, still numb from losing Gunner. Just as I reached down to turn the stereo off, a song by Josh Groban, titled "*To Where You Are*," began to play on the radio. The lyrics touched me deeply as I stood there in the early morning. I truly felt as if Gunner, through some magical way, wanted me to hear that song and, in particular, the words, so I could understand that he was watching over us.

In hindsight, I felt in my heart Gunner's time should have come during Christmas. However, I think he somehow managed to hang on just a little longer for us. Christmas was Gunner's favorite time of the year. Never in my life had I ever seen a dog love to open packages as Gunner did. No, he was not the type of dog that would go under the tree and open any present. But once you handed him a package and he knew it was his, he needed no assistance at all opening the gift.

This year was no different, other than the fact that I silently worried over Gunner's health; but he was not about to let some stupid illness stand in the way of his enjoying Christmas.

After all was said and done, the vets finally believed Gunner had fallen victim to pancreatic cancer. Cathy and I mourned the loss of Gunner for months. From the time I met Cathy, Gunner was a mama's boy. Oh, don't get me wrong. I loved Gunner and he loved me. But from the beginning when Cathy would fly out for a visit and then leave to go back to Massachusetts, I was not the only one moping around the house missing her. Gunner, too, missed her. So, the loss was extremely hard on Cathy. Even the girls, Penny and Panda, just could not seem to get on with their lives. They were depressed with Gunner's passing. Nothing we did seemed to bring them joy anymore. Both the beagles spent hours in their beds, not wanting to go outside and play. Not even the warm rays from the sunshine could get Penny out of her state of depression.

I emailed one of Gunner's breeders to let her know of his passing. She knew of a six-month-old puppy that was Gunner's great grandson, and he was available for adoption. She explained that after a couple had picked the puppy for adoption, the lady decided she was more a cat person, and they let the breeder know that she could put the puppy up for adoption again. Several weeks after Gunner passed away, I asked to see the puppy. The breeder's friend, Judy, came to our house with him. From the moment I saw the little male beagle get out of the van, he looked like a smaller version of Gunner to me. It was hard to fathom that two beagles could look so much alike. We brought Penny and Panda out in the backyard with the puppy. The little guy raced Penny around the yard, playing with her until Panda finally joined in the action. When I turned to Cathy, she broke down into tears, saying it was just too soon.

Judy was kind enough to understand and kept in touch with me. Finally in February, at our request, Judy drove the little puppy all the way from the East Mountains into the city and left him with us for the day. We took him back to her in the afternoon. Each week, the little puppy would pay us a visit. We were all attempting to see if this was a good fit, not only for us, but for the girls as well. Pretty soon the puppy had a name; we began calling him Tyler on his visits with us.

While Penny took to Tyler right away, Panda wanted very little to do with him. In fact, if she could have, she would have greeted him at the front door, said hello, shut the door in his face, and called that a visit. Panda's cold beagle shoulder never seemed to bother Tyler. Each time he came, he was ready for playtime, whether the girls wanted it or not.

In mid March, Judy brought Tyler to us one last time and left him. He was now officially a member of the Glass family. While he looked just like his great- grandpa, he acted nothing like him. Gunner was always a gentleman, first and foremost. In fact, one of our dear friends, Lisa, who was never a dog lover by nature, told us one Christmas as we sat around the dinner table, "If ever I would have a dog, it would be one just like Gunner. He is the most distinguished dog I have ever known, and he is a gentleman."

I think Lisa summed it up very well. Tyler, on the other hand, did not prescribe to the theory of being a gentleman. In fact, I do not think he had one gentleman gene from Gunner's bloodline. Nonetheless, Tyler brought laughter back into our household. However, that laughter would not last long.

A little less than six months after Gunner's death, on June 11, Cathy's father, Frank, called to explain that he was having, and I quote, "a few stomach problems." Cathy felt she should fly back to Florida to be there when they did exploratory surgery to find out what the problem was. On July 28 that same year, Frank passed away from pancreatic cancer. To say the least, the Glass household was not having a very good year.

Sleepytown Beagles

*A*FTER THE DEATH OF MY mother many years ago at an early age, a good friend stepped in by choice as my adopted mother. I guess if I need to pin a title to her, what always comes to mind is *honorary mother*. Lynn was there to listen to me when I needed to talk. It was she who received a phone call when I sold my first article in New York as a young journalist, and it was she who attended my wedding. Somehow within my lifetime, I have been blessed with both a wonderful biological mother and an exemplary honorary mother.

Nonetheless, along with the title of honorary mother came a certain latitude of "motherly pushing." Oh, I don't mean to imply she would butt into my affairs. However, one issue in particular she felt strongly about: her love for her, as she called them, "grand-beagles." Even when she moved away to California, we kept the line of communication between us intact. I called each week and sent cards, letters, and photos—lots of photos—of her grand-beagles. Never did we have a conversation without her inquiring about how her grand-beagles were.

Everyone, including Lynn, knew I gave voice to our beagles. I was never quite sure why it started or really even how. I assume it was due to the long hours I spent each day working out of a home office with the beagles as my sidekicks. I suppose this afforded me the ability to look at them and intuitively tell what was going on in their minds. People, including fellow dog lovers, asked me on several occasions about my intuitive connections with each of my beagles and, in particular, my connection with Penny. I am not going to give you some hocus-pocus, fancy answer like I could see inside of her, because that simply would not be the truth. All I can say is that I would have strong feelings about certain things concerning each of our beagles. Although this answer is far from the "in thing," it is simply a fact. It was much like what my biological mother would do when I was in my teenage years. When I walked in from school, she would take one look at me and, before I could pour a glass of milk, would ask, "Do you want to talk about it?" On days like these, I learned at an early age to simply chalk it up to mother's intuition. There was simply no other explanation as to how she knew, but she always did.

Therefore, like my mother, I seemed to be able to connect with our beagles on some unknown level. One of my dear friends mentioned to me, after witnessing my interaction with Chelsea and Brandy several times, that I had what she termed "super sentience."

"What in the world is super sentience? And do I need a pill for this condition?"

"No," she replied, laughing at my question. "Simply give thanks for this gift."

"But how and why did I get this?"

"Simply put, Tim, this is a mental clarity that you have about your beagles, an insight, if you will, as to what they are thinking." She waited, as if to allow me time to digest this new information.

"Okay." I was still unsure what this really

meant to my beagles and me.

"We as humans only use a very small portion of our brains. Some individuals, while in a state of meditation, or even in a traumatic situation, can often draw upon this mental clarity, honing into a level of awareness they never knew they had."

While neither meditation nor trauma could account for the connection with my beagles and me, I can only assume my "super sentience," or whatever you want to call it, was a gift just as she said. And I accepted it for that.

After years of giving voice to the beagles in my life, Lynn began calling me a beagle whisperer. Whisperer or not, each beagle had their own voice and personality as I would talk for them and express their feelings, actions, and thoughts. At best, this was entertaining for most of our friends and family, and laughter was the end result—or was it? While the phenomenon between my beagles and me was humorous for most people, for Lynn, I think it was the springboard for what was to come.

For years, I had talked and mused about doing a book about the beagles. God knows I certainly had plenty of material on an ongoing basis, sharing the same household with these lovable characters. Nonetheless, talk is about all I did; never once did I put pen to paper. After many years on the West Coast, Lynn and her husband returned to New Mexico. It was around this time that Lynn really used the "motherly push" technique each chance she could, pushing her platform like a budding politician for her grand-beagles.

"So when are you going to start the beagle books for my grand-beagles?" Lynn would ask, as if her grand-beagles could not possibly survive another day without their very own book series. My personal favorite was, "So, did you start the beagle books yet?"

While my answer was always my standard "no" or "not yet," it took something so powerful and hard hitting to finally move me into action. The event was 9/11, which unfolded while I sat glued to the television, like I am sure most everyone in America was. I wanted to do something, anything that would help. Oh, I went to church, I prayed, and I donated money. However, I wanted to do something more to help the people—anything. While I had to be realistic, with an inoperable back, I felt helpless. Then one night, while I was watching a segment Peter Jennings was doing, he happened to mention how children and even adults around the world were finding it hard to go to sleep at night after 9/11. Truth be known, I, too, would lay awake at night thinking. The events of 9/11 just seemed to have this incredible ability to creep into your mind at quiet times, such as bedtime, and take hold of your mind and thoughts for hours. The only thing that helped me was visualization techniques I had learned many years ago when I was assigned a health article about the benefits of hypnosis.

Suddenly, I begin to formulate an idea. What if I could create a book series that could somehow help millions of children visualize a safe place so they, too, would have a blueprint to go to sleep with. I began researching; and, with the help of our beagles as the main characters, the Sleepy-town Beagle book series came to life. After hours of research and more drafts ending up lining the bottom of my trash can than I care to admit, I started to write the first book while Cathy was staying with her Dad, Frank, during his short illness before his passing. However, I refused to tell anyone. Not even Cathy knew what I was working on at the time. In mid July, at her request, I flew out to Florida to be with Cathy before Frank passed away. When Cathy briefly stepped out of his hospital room, I told Frank about the first book I had started.

"Believe in yourself, Tim," Frank said to me. Oddly, that was the only advice my father-in-law ever gave me, and it was one of the last things we ever talked about before his death. Truth be known, Frank was the only one besides the beagles and my long-time mentor in writing, author Paula Paul, who knew I had started the beagle books.

When I began taking writing classes years ago at the University of New Mexico, the instructors taught many things, from story structure to how to deliver believable dialog. While all those things are needed to be a good writer, I had two instructors who taught the art of reading your manuscript out loud. This was so you could hear how your words flowed together on the page. So, there I was in my office, banging away at the keyboard for hours writing and reading passage after passage from the first book. While I was busy creating the first book in the Sleepytown Beagle book series, the three beagles, Panda in particular, found that they loved being read to. I was never really sure if they just liked to hear their names read out loud or if they simply liked to hear the stories being read to them.

Panda got to the point where, if I took a day off from writing and, more so, reading the book to them, she would climb to the top of our stairs, bark, and run down the hallway to my office. If I did not come up to the office and work on the book, she would return to the edge of our stairs and bark some more. I am not quite sure, but I think Panda was showing the true signs of being either a future agent or one tough boss.

After many drafts, I finally read the first book to Cathy, *Sleepytown Beagles, Panda Meets Ms. Daisy Bloom*, which was inspired by Panda's love for flowers. From her facial expression, Cathy did not seem at all surprised by the book; instead, she seemed pleased that I had finally started the series. I also shared with her the short conversation that I had with her father about the books before his passing. After I explained how our beagles loved being read to, she finally understood why Panda would bark at the top of the stairs on the weekends, wanting me to come up to the office and work.

On Thanksgiving Day, as we all sat around our

dining room table, I decided it was time to break the news to Lynn. I asked if I could read her something as we finished up dinner. After the table was cleared, I grabbed my manuscript and read it to her and her husband (and, of course, the beagles). To say the least, she was thrilled. Finally, her grand-beagles had their book. I tried to explain the process of publishing a book and how the words would be entombed on a page until it was published. She chatted away, ignoring all the details, refusing to listen to the facts that the books may never get published and that, even if they did, there was no guarantee the public would embrace the books and actually buy them.

In August 2006, *Sleepytown Beagles, Panda Meets Ms. Daisy Bloom* was published and released to the public. The first book in the series was a hit with kids. Panda seemed to be an overnight success, at least to the children that read the books. The simple fact was that children around the world could relate to Panda and the things she did. Meanwhile, Penny was every parent's delight on the pages, as she came across with wisdom of the all knowing one. However, as fan mail rolled in after the book was released, I began to notice something I had not predicted. Some adults began to email or write letters saying that they, too, loved the book. While I wrote the book with children in mind, somehow adults also found the story refreshing and helpful.

By the release of the first book, I was already working on the second book in the series, *Sleepytown Beagles, Penny's 4th of July*, and had worked on close to fifty synopses for other titles in the series. Each book had a lesson for the kids and was always against the backdrop of a peaceful, secure place called Sleepytown. The more I wrote, the more the beagles loved to listen to me read the books to them. If I had to set the books aside and work on other projects, the beagles would simply fall asleep at my feet. Only when the skies would darken overhead as a thunderstorm neared did Penny panic and leave the comfort of my office and hearing the books read to her.

One very sad note was that my biological mother didn't live long enough to see this dream become a reality. Nor did a close, dear friend of Cathy's, who lived in Norwood, and who just adored the beagles. I can honestly say that Jennie and her husband Buck adored Penny and Panda. When I moved to Norwood, Jennie opened her arms and heart to yet another beagle, Gunner. When we got the call on Christmas Day of her passing away, we flew back east for the funeral. As we entered the funeral home, there on a large canvas was a display of family photos, and presented along with all the photos of Jennie and her family members were our beagles.

The Pattern

*B*Y THE SUMMER OF 2006, I noticed Penny's ability to deal with Mother Nature and her gift of rain, and loud claps of thunder from the heavens above, became increasingly harder for her to handle. In addition, the fireworks from the Fourth of July were no celebration for Penny. Although I would put her into her wrap, light the bedside lamp, and turn the television on QVC, she would crawl under our bed riddled with fear. Looking back, I think 2006 was a turning point for her. New Mexico was having a wetter-than-normal year; as one storm rolled out, another one would follow on its heels.

During that time, I began to notice a pattern forming. As winter gave way to spring and the heavens opened up with a downpour of rain, and thunderstorms began to rattle overhead, Penny's health seemed to take a noticeable turn for the worse. Maybe Lynn was right about the beagle whisperer thing to a point, or maybe I just had an intuition that the unexplained health issues that manifested themselves were related to the storm seasons and the stress poor Penny was under during those trying times. Looking back, year after year, Penny would be taken to the vet's office shortly after the rainy season started, followed by another more urgent visit by season's end. Penny would usually be placed on a bland diet for her vomiting; other times it meant a hospital stay. Our vet, Dr. H. tried medication to take the edge off those trying times, but Penny's tender stomach would usually rid the medication from her system long before the medication could be of any help.

One thing was for sure: whether her age was making her health less resilient or she simply could no longer tolerate the stress, I felt Penny was reaching a breaking point. The simple task of letting the beagles outside to relieve themselves on rainy nights many times turned into an hour-long event with both Cathy and I standing out in the rain trying to talk to Penny in an attempt to get her to calm down. Penny would pant nervously and pace the backyard, looking upward at the night sky and waiting for the next bolt of lighting to etch its path across the sky. Penny got so apprehensive about the storms, even if the wind blew and no lightning jetted across the sky and there was not a drop of moisture. She would still go from the calm, laid-back beagle into panic mode.

During the height of the 2006 summer storm season, both Cathy and I noticed an outward expression of what all this stress was doing to Penny. Not only was she having her stomach problems, but her beautiful glossy coat would also turn dull, and she would shed. As the season neared its end, tiny white spots of hair formed on her coat. She began looking more like an appaloosa horse with her spots than the beagle she was. However, by fall, as the rain and thunder rolled out of New Mexico, Penny looked five years younger than her actual age, and the tiny spots were gone. Once again, Cathy, Penny, and I breathed a sigh of relief that the storms had come to an end. Again, it was Penny, the oldest, that would lead the others and set the pace with her head held high on our daily walks. While the storm season was taking a rest, Penny was at her best; and so was her health. Many times as I walked the three beagles, people would stop and talk to us. They always assumed Penny was the youngest of the three, as she never showed any signs of aging.

Nevertheless, as the spring of 2007 began to unfold, and the clouds unleashed their fury upon us below, Penny's nerves unraveled as soon as the first storms rolled across the desert sky. This year, unlike the year before, the tiny white spots came early in the spring. However, they were larger; and as the rainy season progressed, the spots multiplied at a startling rate. Cathy called Dr. H., and we took the next available appointment. After a close examination, our vet wanted to do some research on why Penny's coat was changing. I told Dr. H. then that if we could not somehow get a handle on Penny's stress, we would most assuredly lose her. Several days later, Dr. H. called Cathy with a possible reason for why Penny was becoming spotted. She felt it could be a condition called Vitiligo. When Cathy Googled the medical term to get a better understanding of what this odd-sounding medical term was, it seemed there was no hard-core evidence that it was doing anything more than turning our tri-colored beagle into a spotted beagle. Regardless, my intuitive nature and connection to Penny left me feeling more and more like her condition and health, due to the storms, was spinning out of control like a roller coaster on a collision course with destiny.

By the summer, when I would take my break and gather up the leashes for our early morning walk, many times Penny would just not want to go. Normally, just the sight of her leash would get her excited; but on the days she refused to go for a walk, she appeared tired and would just lie in her bed. I tried to convince myself that she was getting older and deserved the right to say no, even to a walk. I also noticed her bright, dark-brown eyes seemed to look cloudy as the days passed. While many things were changing, both in her outward appearance and, I am sure, on the inside, Penny's intelligence remained sharp. Regardless of what her eyes looked like, she still seemed to have 20/20 beagle vision and could still spot a critter a mile away. Her other regular routine habits, such as knowing exactly when I would eat the last bite of food at dinnertime, which was her cue to trot over to my chair to be petted each night, or having lunch with me as I worked in the office upstairs, never changed. Therefore, I assumed my intuition was wrong; Penny was simply slipping into her golden beagle years, and along with it came change, and I needed to accept this.

Furkids Amongst Us

*T*HROUGHOUT MY LIFETIME, I have figured that there are at least three types of dog owners. The first type has a dog as a household employee, per se. The dog is brought home and placed in the yard to watch over the family home and belongings. While the pet is fed and taken for regular checkups at the vet, there simply is no real deep connection between pet and human.

The second type of dog owner is one whose kids or, possibly, spouse has gone and the dog fills the void in the empty nest. The pup and human have a deep connection with one another.

The dog owner without children, with or without a spouse, makes up the third type. Whether the owner has chosen not to have children for medical or whatever reasons, the owner simply cannot have kids. Once again, the family pet fills a much needed gap within the human's life.

It is my personal opinion that the second and third scenarios really have nothing to do with ownership at all. Rather, they have built a relationship with and responsibility to the pet as a parent would, blessed with a child. Love and devotion runs deep on both sides of the relationship channel for both the pet and human. Like with anything in life, there are variations, exceptions, and degrees of ownership from what I described. Nonetheless, I feel that when it comes to the people who are types two and three, their family pet is their furkid. Once again, this is my opinion and simply speculation on my part, but I can only speak from deep within my heart and my belief system of what I have either seen or felt myself. I know having a furkid rather than a pet is in a way like having a child. Granted, I am never talked back to, called into school by the principal, nor required to plan for their college education. Also, my beagles never ask for money or to borrow the car.

I have, however, found that nature has a way

of blindsiding you to the fact that the furkid is no longer a baby, a kid, or a child. In fact, I think even the furkid is blindsided by this. The forever-young syndrome has a way of sneaking up on all of us over a period of time. I speculate that this could be why so many of us are so bewildered when illness or death occurs. Take, for example, when an elderly person lives a long productive life and we know their years are numbered. When old age and illness sets in, we as humans attempt to prepare ourselves as best we can for what we know can and will someday happen. This rite of passage, while painful for those left behind, is something we can see outwardly as someone grows older.

In contrast to this, the furkid begins to age and manages to overtake us in dog years. You have assumed the role of parent, have provided the best environment and care for your furkid, and do not take your responsibility lightly. Nevertheless, neither you nor the furkid really seem to acknowledge this change as the hands of time slip by. Once again, I speak from the heart and from my own experience, not only with Penny, but also with Gunner and the three beloved beagles that came before him. I was the provider, I was the caregiver, I was the one who they ran to when they were frightened, I was the parent figure of a furkid. Their facial expressions of child-like wonder as they watched whatever I was doing, along with a host of other things, helped reinforce this on a daily basis.

When Penny's illness worsened, the face that looked back at me for guidance and help was still that of my scared, frightened little furkid. Furthermore, she had complete trust that Cathy and I would do what was right for her. I know all too well that many people just cannot understand this deep love and devotion. Therefore, when Penny's illness hit home, Cathy and I noticed some people just could not comprehend the amount of pain we were going through. The fact is, they believed Penny was nothing more than an animal. For pet owners such as us, we remember that for years we have filled the shoes of a parent for this furkid; therefore, the illness, or even death, feels much the same as if we had a sick child, or had lost a child. The simple fact is love is love; it does not distinguish between two legs and four.

Many people who are in the same situation that Cathy and I were in with Penny are simply afraid to admit their feelings to friends and family, leaving them to deal with the pet's illness or death without a solid support system; the kind of system that would be available if the illness involved a child, spouse, or other close family member. For this very reason, I pitched an article on pet loss to OurDogHouse.com for their global newsletter. While the newsletter usually has a more upbeat slant to it with articles about pets to help them and their owners, I truly felt this article was needed to help owners deal with loss. It took only a few days before the owner of OurDogHouse gave a green light to my article. I began drafting my article, titled *Hard to Say Good Bye*, in late August for the October newsletter.

As summer neared its end, it was evident to me that Penny was not just moving into her golden beagle years; rather, she was fighting some unknown villain from within. While Cathy and I faced Penny's illness, thank God we had a wonderful support group of beagle owners and many friends and family members that understood what we (and even Penny) were going through at this difficult time.

On Friday, October 12, as I always did on my break, I got the leashes out for our morning walk and said that magical word in our household,

"Walkies." Panda and Tyler ran to my side and I hooked them up. Looking around, Penny was nowhere to be found. I called her name; however, she did not come. After hooking Panda and Tyler up, I looked for Penny. I found her sleeping in her bed and woke her up. While holding up her leash and showing it to her, I said, "Walkies," once again. Lifting her head, she looked at her leash with sadness. Her eyes expressed, "Sorry, but once again, not today. You'll have to go it alone without me, Dad."

After our morning walk, Penny, when she did stay at home, would usually greet us at the front door. Today, as I opened the door, our foyer was empty. Penny was not there waiting for our return. I checked on her, and she was still in her bed sleeping. While on the surface I wanted so much to believe that she was just tired, for some reason in my gut I knew today was different. I can't really explain why I felt there was more to her lethargic behavior. I called Cathy at her office, and we thought maybe if we waited a while, Penny would bounce back like she had so many times before.

However, on the weekend, Penny got sick after eating her kibble. We knew at times like this we were to give Penny prescription diet food, and we always had it on hand; so we tried that. Nonetheless, it too did not agree with Penny's tender tummy. We called Dr. H., who felt it was possible that her pancreas was flaring up again. She made several suggestions to Cathy for Penny's dinners. Penny would manage one bite of each thing we tried but then she would get sick. It was much like a human who ate something that did not agree with her or him and then would refuse to eat it again. Penny seemed to associate this with whatever bit of food we gave her that made her sick. Thus, in turn, she would refuse to eat it again.

On Monday, October 15, we called our vet, explaining that Penny was not any better, nor was she eating. We took her into the vet's office that morning. Dr. H. did a thorough exam of Penny, even drawing blood, and she asked to keep her at the hospital, where they would start her on IV fluids and medication. Once again, Penny and her favorite blanket took up temporary residency at our vet's hospital, with Cathy and me calling every couple of hours to check on her condition.

On Tuesday, after the blood test came back,

Dr. H. called and suggested that we do an ultrasound and possibly a liver biopsy due to elevations of something in Penny's blood. Our options were to wait until Thursday or drive to Santa Fe, New Mexico, on Wednesday and have the tests done there. We opted to have the test done as soon as possible. Dr. H. quickly called in a referral with the doctor in Santa Fe, and we locked in an appointment for the next day, Wednesday, October 17, at 10 a.m.

For me, the ultrasound equaled hope in the form of the story it would reveal to the medical professionals and to us. My hope was that once they could see within Penny's body and know just what the problem was, then they could simply fix it or remove it. So while I was still very worried, I allowed myself the luxury of this feeling of hope.

Late Tuesday evening, we were able pick up Penny from our vet and keep her overnight, so we would be able to have an early start first thing Wednesday morning to make our pilgrimage to Santa Fe. When Cathy and I picked Penny up, she did not bounce out to greet us as she had always done in the past. She looked haggard and worn down by whatever was ailing her. Nonetheless, we greeted her with open arms and lots of love. Upon arriving home with Penny and her bag full of medications, we both noticed Panda and Tyler acting up more than usual. Their behavior reminded us of when a family has one child who is very sick; usually the other children often begin to act up to get attention. Cathy and I did our very best to give Panda and Tyler the attention they needed while caring for Penny; however, it just did not do the trick. Panda and Tyler continued to do anything and everything they could to get our attention, or maybe to get our minds off of what was going on with Penny.

That night we tried to get Penny to eat; but, at best, she ate only a small bite and turned away from any additional offering. My heart physically ached for her. I wanted her to be better, and my hope was coming tomorrow in the form of the ultrasound. I knew it would magically give us the answers we so desperately needed. Before going to bed, I sent out an email to all our family and friends, asking them to please say a prayer for Penny. Cathy did the same, and also added a prayer request on the beagle list.

Trip of Hope

O N WEDNESDAY, OCTOBER 17, Cathy and I rolled out of bed before the sun came up over the Sandia Mountains. Neither of us had really slept well, listening in case Penny needed us during the night. Her breathing was rapid and labored throughout the night. However, I can remember while laying there in the darkness that each time there would be a short period when I could not hear her breathing, I feared the worse.

That morning, I took Penny out in our backyard. While I knew she was happy to be home and with us, I also knew that she was not herself as she wandered through the grass aimlessly. It reminded me of an expression used by the Hopi Indians I had heard often as a kid, *Koyaanis-qatsi*, which means "life out of balance."

Whatever was happening to our Penny was throwing her life and her health out of balance and harmony. But I knew, or at least prayed, that was about to change with our trip to Santa Fe—I knew it.

I pulled the back seats down in our Toyota 4-Runner and added a sheet and two comfy beagle beds. I reasoned that this way Penny could pick the bed of her choice that would allow her to be the most comfortable on our long trip. I packed fresh water and some food for Penny and us to snack on for our long drive home after the ultrasound test and liver biopsy was done. In my mind, after the test we would all be able to take a much-needed sigh of relief and celebrate. When Penny was in the back of our 4-Runner, Cathy fed Panda and Tyler, since Penny was not allowed to have even her small bite of food before the test.

"We're going for bye-byes," I said to Penny, hoping it would cheer her up a little as it usually did. Unfortunately, even the promise of a road trip did nothing for Penny. As I sat in the driver's seat waiting for Cathy, I talked to Penny, telling her that we were going to drive up to Santa Fe, New Mexico, where they had an ultrasound machine, so we could find out what was wrong. The look on her face that morning as she looked back at me is still etched in my mind as one of child-like faith and complete trust in me. I was going to get her to someplace, wherever that place was, and they would help her get out of this pain she was in; and that was my goal.

Cathy finished feeding Panda and Tyler, and we headed off for Santa Fe for the much-needed answers we had prayed for.

Road Trip

*H*EADING NORTH OUT of Albuquerque, we had a little less than a two-hour drive to get to the vet, who was located just outside of Santa Fe. Cathy quickly adjusted the radio station to Penny's liking. Yes, each of our beagles had their own taste in music. Tyler liked his country tunes, and Panda was into classical jazz to the point where, if we drove and listened to country too long, she became a wild woman in the backseat. Penny, however, loved her easy listening station and, I think, was silently addicted to the Delilah show. So, with Magic 99.5 FM tuned in and softly playing in the background, we headed to Santa Fe.

Penny fared well on the long drive, sleeping

most of the way there. I could not help thinking that under normal circumstances and health, Penny would have loved the road trip. In fact, Cathy and I had learned to spell the words "bye-bye" around the beagles. We could never say the words unless we made good on the promise that we were actually going someplace with them. If we did slip, which happened every once in a while, all the beagles would gather at the garage door in one big happy wag fest, waiting to go on a road trip. However, today was very different. Every couple of minutes, I found myself looking in the rearview mirror to check on Penny. Occasionally, she would get up from one bed and move to the other. Nonetheless, the look on her face was still that of a tired, haggard beagle.

When we finally arrived at the Santa Fe vet's office, we were told that it was extremely important not to let Penny relieve herself, having something to do with her bladder or kidneys being full or at least having something in them. There we were on a chilly morning after a long drive, and poor Penny couldn't even relieve herself. I carried her into the office, figuring that would help. There Penny, Cathy, and I sat alone in a large lobby, waiting. I went back outside and carried one of Penny's beds inside for her, but she would not lie down in it. So I carried her back out to the 4-Runner, and Cathy waited in the vehicle with her while I sat in the lobby and waited to be called.

Finally, an older gentleman walked out into the lobby and called my name. He asked me to sit down at a small table where he began asking me questions and writing down my answers. As he wrote, I kept thinking to myself, why on earth don't we just get in there to the ultrasound machine and get this going so we can have the real answers to this puzzle? Four double-sided pages of questions later, they were ready for Penny; so I went out and carried her back in. Much to our relief, Mike, the veterinarian and Naomi, the sonographer explained to Cathy and me that we could be in the room with Penny as they did the ultrasound. We were ushered into a small, dimly lit room equipped with a monitor and what looked like a computer and another machine hooked up to it. Off to one side of the room was a small aluminum table where they placed a V-shaped pillow block. I was told to lift Penny and place her on her left side on the pillow block.

I looked at Cathy, as both of us knew Penny would normally struggle against anyone trying to place her in that position, no less up on a table. However, Penny was too weak to fight, and she allowed me to place her carefully into the cradle-shaped pillow. With Penny now in place on the table, the vet technician warmed up the ultra-sound machine gel, and then Naomi gently rubbed it all over Penny's belly and side. The combination of the warmth from the gel and the massage by the compassionate sonographer made Penny really kick back and enjoy this moment in time. For a brief second, I could have easily forgotten why we were all really there and simply thought we were at the beagle day spa. However, all of us, including Penny, were here for a task, a search-and-find mission per se; a mission, I prayed silently to myself, that would help us all help her.

With the gel now in place, Naomi turned and grabbed a wand-shaped object and began to rub that over Penny's side and belly. Cathy took up her position by Penny's head, all the while talking softly to Penny to keep her calm. I was to hold Penny's back legs, which also allowed me to have a birds-eye view of the monitor as the ultrasound machine peered inside Penny. Naomi was extremely gentle with Penny as she ran this wand-shaped head over her side and tummy.

"This right side of her pancreas," she explained, turning to me, "is a little inflamed."

Inflamed, I thought to myself. We can handle inflamed; how bad could that be? It sounded treatable. Moving the wand around, she pointed to the monitor and traced the image with her fingertip on the screen.

"This is her liver——" she said. I noticed her narration seemed to abruptly come to a stop, almost mid sentence, as she focused her complete attention on the screen and ran the wand back and forth over Penny's liver.

"Notice how enlarged it is. There is also a large lump on the bottom," she said, pointing to the screen once again. The lump appeared to be a bellow-shaped object attached to the bottom of Penny's liver. Oddly, I felt like I had the same size lump forming in my throat and in the pit of my stomach. Nevertheless, I assured myself that a lump should be something they could remove, or at least I prayed they could. I found myself wishing she had an eraser on the tip of that wand and could simply just erase that lump from

Penny's insides. The sonographer hovered over the liver then moved on to the next organ.

"This is her spine; it is extremely enlarged, too."

As she hovered over Penny's spleen, I noticed just how grossly oversized the organ was. Somewhere between Penny's liver and spleen, I felt as if my hopes had managed to get that same slippery gel smeared all over them. Little by little, image by image, my hopes slipped away. I felt like a child looking at a bad report card for the first time, wanting to take a pen and change the grade, as if that would somehow change the outcome. This was our trip of hope, I reminded myself silently; this was not supposed to be happening.

I assume this kind of thinking is partly due to my persona, which has never changed through the years. Once, as a young student at the University of New Mexico, I had a professor hold up a glass partly filled with water to the class.

"Describe this," he said to the class. One student went into a complete description of the composition of glass then moved onto the water. The professor just smiled.

"A little beyond what I was wanting, Mr.

Baca."

"A glass half full," I blurted out.

"Good, Mr. Glass. Anyone else?"

"A glass half empty," a girl in the back of the room said.

So I had to hold onto the theory of the glass being half full, a more positive way of looking at things, where Penny's health was concerned. After all, I was not a medical doctor; therefore, while the images of Penny's organs seemed upsetting to Cathy and me, somehow they were going to find a way to make our Penny better. I had to hold onto that thought, regardless of what I was seeing on that screen and feeling deep in my gut.

At this point, the sonographer had Cathy and I turn Penny onto her back as she traced more of Penny's internal organs.

"Let's take a look at the other side of the pancreas." Then turning to the medical team in the room, she said, "We have multi-organ involvement here." The dialog from the medical team, while looking at Penny beyond the point where her liver came into view on the tiny screen, could have been described with one word: enlarged. Penny's liver, spine, and one side of her pancreas were extremely enlarged. Whatever all these images meant, it did not sound good to me.

The sonographer continued running the wand over Penny, looking at her kidneys. Thank God, they looked good. Once she was satisfied that she had all the images she needed, she wiped the gel off Penny's tummy and instructed me to lift her off the table. As we stood there in the dimly lit room, I heard a printer come to life in the back of the room.

The reality of all this was more than I could handle. While I tried to keep a strong, positive look on my face, I knew this was for Cathy and Penny's sake. Inside, I was scared. I wanted to get out of the exam room. I needed fresh air, fresh anything at this point. I asked if I could take Penny for a walk and let her relieve herself. They explained that they first needed to take a blood test to make sure Penny could withstand a liver biopsy. After the quick blood test, I took Penny for a walk while they waited to see if Penny's blood platelets would clot correctly. I needed to get out of there, and I felt Penny did, too. As I took her for a walk, I tried to assure Penny, and myself, that something could and would be done.

My mind was a blur as one thought after another raced through it like a locomotive coming down a track, both positive and negative. I prayed as we walked.

I looked down at Penny. Here we were in a strange place, which, under normal circumstances, would have had Penny's adrenalin pumping with all the new sights, smells, and sounds. However, Penny was worn down; her earthly body was failing her. She simply ambled alongside me as we walked. Gone was her excitement; gone was her incredible stride that I loved so much. God, I wanted to run away, as if by running, Penny and I could somehow magically manage to outrun this illness. But there was no way of running away from what was within her. I knelt down and held Penny's head up to me, looking at her sad eyes.

"You've got to fight this, Penny," I told her, as I pet her soft head and ears. Just then, my cell phone rang. It was Cathy calling from the office; they wanted us back inside.

As I entered the room, I noticed Cathy's eyes were red and swollen as she talked to the team of medical professionals. The fact is, they could not do the liver biopsy; not today, as Penny's platelets were "iffy," to say the least. Added to this equation was the danger of the long-distance drive back to Albuquerque. The stretch of I-25 we had to travel was a no man's land, just highway for miles stretched out like a thin ribbon across a vast mesa. With Penny's platelets the way they were, if she started to bleed, we would be miles and miles away from any help, and she could bleed to death. We were instructed to head directly to our vet in Albuquerque with the printouts of the ultrasound. She requested that they redo the blood test there and send it off to an out-of-state lab. We made a tentative appointment for the next day for the biopsy to be done in the Albuquerque area at 10 a.m. However, everything hung on one thing, and that was Penny's blood test and her platelets. We quickly paid our bill, gathered everything up, and headed back to Albuquerque.

A few hours later, and miles away from the Santa Fe vet, we sat waiting in our vet's lobby as they drew Penny's blood and prepared to ship the test to the lab. Finally, it was time for us all to head back home. We were physically and emotionally spent. I carried Penny into the house and placed her gently onto her bed. When I went back outside to unload the truck, I grabbed the food I had packed and realized we never touched a bit of it.

Cathy was given an outline of what we could try to feed Penny. Still, at best, she would take her usual bite of something, get sick, and refuse it the second time. Nonetheless, I kept telling myself that there was still hope tomorrow, once they got her blood test back and we could have the liver biopsy done.

October 18th

THURSDAY MORNING, OCTOBER 18, before I opened my eyes, I prayed for a miracle that somehow Penny would be all better. However, her fever was raging on, and her breathing was still rapid. Cathy and I went about the business of preparing things for taking her in for her liver biopsy. By nine o'clock, Cathy and I had not received a call from either of the vets to tell us whether or not Penny would be able to make it through the liver biopsy. By 9:20, Cathy decided to call Dr. H. I grabbed my cell phone and put in a call to Naomi, the sonographer in Santa Fe, but only got her voicemail. Meanwhile, Cathy learned that our vet was consulting with an internal medicine vet about Penny. We didn't know whether we were staying or going; we were in a holding pattern hovering somewhere between hope and despair. Seconds ticked away, seeming like minutes; minutes seemed like hours until my cell phone rang.

The sonographer from Santa Fe explained to me that Penny would not be able to survive the biopsy; her blood platelets told the same exact story they had the day before. The liver biopsy would probably cause Penny to bleed excessively; and, more than likely, she would bleed to death before they would be able to stop it. The sonographer explained that Dr. H. was consulting an internal medicine doctor, and that there were treatments such as chemotherapy available for dogs. Then she said the word "lymphoma," and from that point on, I simply answered yes to everything she said in a somewhat robotic matter. In fact, from then on, I could not tell you what she really said. At some point, I merely disconnected our call. My mind was on overload and simply could no longer deal with the information she was offering me.

I sat upstairs in my office, numb, and still holding my cell phone when our home phone rang. I heard Cathy take the call. Slowly, I walked downstairs into our bedroom where Penny lay in her bed. I could see how much pain she was in. I sat down beside her bed. Holding her head and petting her, I told her that I understood. If she needed to go, Cathy and I would miss her, but we would be okay. I am a firm believer that many times both humans and pets hold on to life, waiting for the acceptance of those of us that will be left behind.

I walked slowly out of the room, wiping the tears from my eyes, and stood by Cathy's side until she was done talking to our vet. After she hung up and cried, she explained to me that while chemo was an option, we may or may not even have a year left with Penny. Dr. H. asked Cathy and I to consider the quality of life that Penny would be left with. Regardless, our vet did want to start Penny on another drug, something more powerful than the other drugs lining our kitchen counter. I grabbed my keys and told Cathy to call them back to tell them I was on my way to pick up whatever this was. After returning home, I gave Penny the new prescription, which seemed to make her rebound. However, the rebound was short lived, lasting only a few hours, until she, once again, began ridding the medicine from her system.

I had to face it; I had to resolve myself to the fact that we were losing our Penny. Her earthly form was failing her at a rapid, painful rate. Now, part of me prayed she would simply close her eyes, drift off into a peaceful sleep, and pass away on her own, so we would not have to make the decision for her.

Dr. H. called back later that day to check in on Penny. She explained our plan for creating a kind of hospice care for Penny as long as we could. Cathy and I would know when the time would be.

It's Time to Go

$\mathcal{A}$S I LOOKED AT PENNY LYING in her bed, I found that in the realization of her condition, the pain was almost unbearable. I found the only way I could deal with the pain and hurt that lay before me was to picture her on her back, basking in the glow of the warm New Mexico sunshine, looking skyward and dreaming as she had done so many days before. I allowed myself the luxury to further wonder just what it was that always attracted Penny to gaze for sometimes an hour or more at the beautiful blue canvas sky above her as God managed to sculpt beautiful white fluffy clouds of all shapes and sizes.

Suddenly, a healing thought crossed my mind and crept into the depths of my heart. I pictured

Penny soaring across those blue skies above, free from the pain, free from this illness, and free from any fear. This was the way I wanted to think of our Penny, this was the way I wanted to remember her. Denial, I guess, could be setting in as I refused to see Penny as she was, lying there ill in her bed, or walking aimlessly across our backyard. Maybe this thought was my mental crutch, because as time and the illness wore on, it was what I held onto.

Along with this mental visualization, I found myself associating with and focusing once again on a song to help me through these troubled times. For whatever reason, this song kept popping into my head. The song was written by Diane Warren, one of music industry's most prolific songwriters and composers. Titled *There You'll Be*, it was recorded and released in 2001 for the soundtrack of the movie, "Pearl Harbor." To me, those lyrics were all so fitting—lyrics such as "In my dreams I'll always see you soar above the sky," or "I was blessed to get to have you in my life." It was as if Ms. Warren somehow magically peered into my heart at this point in time and wrote this song for Penny and me. Of course, I know this is not true, and I am sure that, for many people who love that song, they too can find a connection to it. Nevertheless, it helped in my visualization of Penny.

Why I allowed this visualization to enter into my mind and heart I am really not sure, even to this day. I simply assume death or dying does not come easy for man or beast. Nor does acceptance of the death of a loved one; and again, it does not matter whether there are four legs or two. Death is death. It marks the end of a birth here on this earth and, further, the end of what we have come to know for so many years as a life we have known and loved.

While many people, I assume, feel death is the final act of living, I firmly believe there is more to life than just what we have here on this earth, even for our beloved pets. I would also agree Penny had earned the right to passage for going on to a much better place than Cathy or I could offer her here on earth. I knew I hurt for myself, Cathy, and even Panda and Tyler. It is always us, the ones left behind, that the tears fall for. I knew Penny would soon be beyond this lifetime on a journey only she could take; neither Cathy nor I could be by her side as we had always been. Penny would be out of this horrific pain that riddled her body. Nevertheless, it was extremely hard for us to let go. To add to this dilemma, I think Penny fought to stay with us and hold onto what she knew. It was as if with one painful breath she wanted to be here with the family she had grown up with, and with the next breath wanted to let go for a promise of what was to come.

As nightfall came upon us, there was a painful resemblance of normalcy. Cathy prepared Panda and Tyler's meals as she always did. Excitement filled our kitchen for Panda and Tyler as they stood and watched Cathy carry their food bowls to their special spots where each one ate. It was extremely heartbreaking to notice the void where Penny's stand for her bowl once sat on the kitchen floor.

The following day, Penny ate a little food and took her medicine. I wondered for a brief moment if, possibly, we had been blessed with a miracle. I prayed that the doctors and all their equipment were wrong. Several minutes later, Penny was outside vomiting her meds up. Faced with reality once again, I knelt by her side and held her until the retching ceased.

Mid-morning, our vet called; we reported

Penny's present condition to her, and the fact that she was unable to keep anything down, including her meds. There was a long silence on the line. After a few seconds, Dr. H. explained to us both that the final decision was up to us, but we needed to think of the quality of life and the pain Penny was in. Cathy and I asked to call her back after we talked.

Cathy and I went outside in our backyard and talked and cried. However, by the end of the conversation, we had reached the conclusion that to keep Penny here with us was selfish, considering Penny's prognosis. At best, we would be buying days with her; nonetheless, those would be painful days for Penny and all of us. We called the vet back, and she offered us two options: we could drop Penny off and they would sedate her until they could put her down, or we could stay with her. Both Cathy and I knew without saying a word to each other that we needed to be by Penny's side. We told the vet that we wanted to stay with Penny and, in fact, be with her in the room when they put her down. Dr. H. attempted to advise against it, but neither Cathy nor I would listen. We insisted that we wanted to be by her side. We were told to bring her in at 4:00 that afternoon.

We had a few hours to wait. Both Cathy and I took Penny out back to relieve her. As we both sat on our patio, Penny laid down in the grass, rolled onto her back, and gazed up into the sky in her usual daydream state. It was a beautiful, warm fall day. We both sat there watching her as she took in the warm New Mexico sunshine. I reached over for Cathy's hand as I saw the tears streaming down her face. If we had not known Penny's condition, this day would have been perfect. However, our hearts were breaking. On one hand, we knew that today we would have to say goodbye, but on the other, we knew that she would finally be out of pain.

As a breeze picked up, we called Penny, Panda, and Tyler to come inside the house. Penny went back to bed in our bedroom. As the clock ticked away and it got close to the time we needed to leave, Penny came out of the bedroom by herself, walked over to me as I sat on the loveseat in our den, and wanted me to pet her. As I stroked her soft coat, I looked over at Cathy—Penny had not done this since she took ill. Then after about ten minutes, she walked around and sat in front of me, looking straight at me as if saying, Okay, Dad, it's time for me to go. Oddly enough, we looked at the clock on the mantel and it was.

Penny's Journey

I COULD FEEL AND even see my body moving, performing the tasks that needed to be done. With each movement, I felt myself wanting to hold back. In fact, it felt as if I was moving in a slow, methodical motion as I loaded Penny's bed into the back of our 4-Runner.

"Why?" I cried out. "Why, God?" Shaking my head, I straightened Penny's blankets before going back into the house to get her for what would be her final road trip to the vet. As I wiped the tears from my eyes, I entered our house.

"Are we ready?" God, of all the stupid questions I could possibly utter from my mouth, I thought to myself. Could anyone really be ready to do what Cathy, I, or even Penny had to do next? The answer was no. Nonetheless, within a few minutes we were all loaded into the 4-Runner and traveling to the east side of Albuquerque. I found it hard to look at Penny on the trip, even though I wanted to know she was okay. Neither Cathy nor I really said much.

Once at the vet's office, I stopped the truck and we all just sat there, paralyzed by fear and sadness. It was Penny who stood up first and walked slowly toward the front seat. Like it or not, I knew I had to do this. I grabbed the keys from the ignition. Getting out, I picked Penny up and carried her into the lobby. We were taken into a room right away.

When Dr. H. entered the exam room, I asked her to please give Penny a complete exam once more. If there was any hope, even a shred, I wanted to give Penny every chance in the world. She gave Penny a complete exam, going over every inch of her.

"Tim, Cathy, her fever has spiked. If I can tell you anything at all, I can simply tell you her condition has worsened."

This was not the answer I was hoping for. At that point, Cathy and I gave a go-ahead nod in place of the words that just seemed to catch in a knot in our throats.

"We will start by giving her a sedative; this will relax her first." They gave Penny the shot and I left the room to go get Penny's bed. When I came back to the exam room, I found Cathy holding Penny on her lap. Penny's liver was so damaged from the cancer, and the sedative weakened her to the point that she could not sit on her own. I put the bed on the floor in the exam room, picked Penny up, and laid her down onto it. Cathy and I got down on the floor and pet Penny. At several points, Penny's breathing completely ceased for minutes. I prayed she would just let go on her own and pass on. However, fighting the inevitable, Penny would pull another labored breath of life into her lungs.

Five minutes before 5 p.m., the door to the exam room opened and Dr. H. asked, once again, if both of us were sure we wanted to stay with Penny. We both said yes. In our hearts it wasn't even a question of *if* we should stay; we *knew* we wanted to be by her side. We lifted Penny and her bed onto the exam table.

"This will only take seconds," Dr. H. said, looking at both Cathy and I once again.

"Penny, go to Gunner," I said, as our doctor

inserted the needle. "Don't fight it. Mommy and I will be okay. Just go to Gunner and we will be with you someday."

Penny only took three breaths before she passed over to the other side. Her body relaxed and her eyes opened; she was at peace. Penny was no longer fighting this battle with cancer. I knew in my heart at that very moment that she was finally free. She was where she really always dreamed of being—soaring across the sky like the words to the song *"There You'll Be."*

"You guys stay here as long as you need," Dr. H. said as she hugged us both. "You did the right thing for Penny; trust me, you did."

Cathy and I gently held Penny and softly talked to her for several minutes.

"She's no longer in that body, sweetheart," I said finally, holding Cathy in my arms.

"I know," she sobbed, trying to wipe the continuous flow of tears away.

We stepped outside into the lobby. Cathy sat down and exhaled. She was emotionally drained. I quickly ran out to our truck. I had brought a favorite toy of Penny's that I had given her several Christmases ago. It was a little white stuffed lamb, which we had nicknamed Baa Baa.

Penny loved the toy and would sleep with it in her bed each night. For whatever reason, we could tell that this was something Penny seemed to treasure. Knowing we were going to have Penny cremated, I thought it was best that Baa Baa take the journey with Penny. I stepped back into the room with Penny as Dr. H. was placing a blanket on her.

"Can we put this with her? It was her favorite toy," I said holding Baa Baa out. Without a word, our teary-eyed vet lifted Penny's front leg and stuck the toy under it. I stayed in the room by Penny's side in the silence by myself. I had a sudden urge to scoop her up into my arms and carry her body out into the sunshine that I knew she loved so much. Then I realized that both Penny and Baa Baa were already there, only on a much higher level. There Penny would be forever in the brilliant glow of her sunbeam.

"Penny, I feel so blessed to have been a part of your life. You taught me so very much about life, but mostly about living. You loved without any request from anyone, or us. No matter what type of day Mommy or I was having. It never mattered to you if we felt like we were on top of the world or at the bottom of the pile. The fact is, your love

127

was unconditional and always there for us."

I turned away and walked toward the door to leave. Just as I took hold of the door handle, I turned back and looked at Penny one last time.

"Goodbye, sweet Penny, until we meet again. I love you."

Cathy and I made the arrangements for the cremation and then cried our way back home. After we pulled into the garage, we just sat there holding each other. When we finally entered our home, Tyler and Panda already seemed to be in a state of grief. I truly believe that animals have a much better grasp on death than we humans realize. Suddenly, we had been reduced from a family of five to a family of four. The wound of our loss was laid wide open and the pain was quite evident.

The Dash

*A*FTER THE PASSING OF A human or a pet, I think it is only natural that most of us tend to reflect upon the lives of those who have departed. I believe this is part of the natural grieving process. Therefore, after Penny passed on, I found myself recalling the memorial service for my father-in-law. During Frank's funeral, the minister shared with everyone a beautiful story he had once heard, called "The Dash." He began by asking us all a rhetorical question.

"When walking by a gravestone in a cemetery, can any of you recall the small, very insignificant thing that goes along with the date of birth and the date of death on a headstone?"

I sat there, probably like most at the memorial

service, and tried to think of what the minister was referring to, and I honestly had no clue.

"The dash—that small mark. That is what I am talking about," he said, attempting to make eye contact with everyone at the crowded memorial service. "The fact is, it hardly gets a second thought. Most people look at the date a person is born and then their eyes travel to the date the person died."

Okay, I thought to myself, the dash. What in the world are we doing here talking about a dash on a headstone? My father-in-law, Cathy's father, just passed away and this is his memorial service, for God's sake. What does a dash have to do with my father-in-law?

"The dash, my friends," he hesitated, looking around from face to face, "is one of the most important parts of a person's very existence here on this earth. You see, the dash is a represent-tation of the life that person lived. While the symbol in itself is small, I agree, and very unnoticeable on a grave marker, it is the dash that is one of the most important things."

For the first time in my life, I really gave that little dash a thought. I realized how important it was and, further, what I wanted people in my life, or those who I have touched in some way, to remember me and my dash as.

I felt that Penny's dash could have been represented as one long line stretching for miles. This little thirty-pound beagle with a ninety-pound heart of gold had managed to touch so many people in her lifetime, both in person and on the pages of the Sleepytown Beagle books. Most humans could take a lesson from her, myself included.

The fact is, Penny lived her life to the fullest extent. Most importantly, she managed to enjoy life here on this earth. If ever there was a dog who truly understood total balance and alignment with life, Penny was that pup! Another thing I think that added to her rosy persona was the fact that Penny was a beagle with a smile. Whether she was awake or sleeping, Penny's lips formed a beautiful smile that framed her beagle girl face. It was also a smile that could brighten even the darkest days. Then there were her hours of laying in the glow of her beloved sunbeam, staring upward into the sky and watching the clouds above her dance across the southwestern skies to the melody of wind chimes that hung on the back porch. There she would lie in our backyard in an almost meditative state. I found myself wondering if this, in and of itself, was Penny's secret to the full and rewarding life she had led. This beagle, for whatever reason, managed to set aside time to meditate on something beyond this world each and every day. One could only speculate as to what it was that drew Penny's attention skyward each and every day for hours, and what it really meant to her and to her life. However, in my heart, it was Penny's key to a happy life.

Penny had painted a beautiful portrait of "The Dash" on the canvas of life that could be neither overlooked nor ignored. The dash she left behind was an incredible accomplishment for a beagle.

The Unexplained

*F*OR MANY PEOPLE, WHAT happened next could possibly be explained as wishful thinking or just plain craziness, I guess. Nevertheless, throughout the years, readers of my well-over-300 published manuscripts have known me to be honest with them, as I tell them all I know. Furthermore, they expect me to be honest enough to tell them when I have no idea. While I assume some authors might omit this next part of the story for fear of sounding unbelievable, I feel it is very important to the overall story.

During the next few days that followed Penny's death, both Cathy and I had a few unexplained occurrences around the house that just did not add up. We were not strangers to this, as some odd, unexplained things happened after Gunner's passing. When Gunner passed away, Cathy and I would be sitting in our den on the loveseat when we would hear a scratch at the backdoor. The first time I heard the scratching I jumped up to find nothing, not even a beagle at the backdoor. After a few more times, Cathy and I would simply turn around on the loveseat to see nothing but a door. Before Gunner's passing, the scratching was his signal to us that he needed go outside.

The evening after Penny's passing, Cathy and I were sitting in our den on the loveseat. The loss of Penny hung like a dark cloud in the room over the complete household. I had just finished a long-distance phone call with Lynn, my honorary mom, who had been calling us each and every day to check on Penny, her grand-beagle, before her passing—and she kept the calling up afterward to check on us. Within seconds of hanging up on the call, Panda walked over to my side of the loveseat wanting to be petted, which was never something Panda liked. Panda was just not the type of dog who liked to be petted; and if one of us did pet her, she would only allow it for a few seconds and would then walk away.

However, that evening, Panda stood and allowed me to pet her. While this was unusual, to say the least, the oddest thing was the way she was backing up and moving forward to get me to pet her. When Penny was alive she had somehow worked out a method to her benefit whereby she would direct the person's hand to the very spot she wanted. She would always begin by having you pet her neck, and then, by going forward, she would manage to get you to pet her shoulders. This back-and-forth movement did not stop until she was petted all the way down. Then she would back around and work her way back up to her neck. As Penny would back up, I would make a beeping sound with my mouth that sounded much like one of those large trucks or moving construction equipment, which I am sure everyone has heard at least once in their lifetime.

As I began to pet Panda that evening, I looked over at Cathy and shrugged my shoulders in bewilderment, knowing that petting was something Panda never liked. As I pet Panda, she began to move forward every few minutes just as Penny always had. To say the least, it was as if we suddenly had a visitor from beyond. The Native American Indians would call this phenomena *shapeshifting.* Many years ago, as legend has it, the Sioux warriors used shapeshifting to become better at feeding their families by transforming themselves into buffalo. This transformation was to make them excellent hunters, history tells us. Shapeshifting seems to have no borders when it comes to this belief. China, Japan, and Korea are just a few of the many countries with cultures that believe in this. Today, I assume this ancient belief system would be termed folklore.

No matter what you want to label it, Panda was acting out of character. I guess, for lack of a better explanation, maybe she simply missed her sister and needed contact. However, I am confused as to why the forward movement came into play, or why she turned exactly as Penny had always done. Furthermore, the petting episodes continued. Though it didn't happen every day, out of the blue, there Cathy and I would be, and Panda would wake up from a sleep and walk over and want to be petted as Penny had.

Petting, however, was not the only thing that happened that really had no clear-cut explanation. One day, Cathy and I were hanging curtains in our bedroom. Panda and Tyler were fast asleep in their beds when I heard what sounded like a dog's squeaky toy. For fear of sounding like I had lost my mind, I said nothing at first. Needless to say, it happened again.

"Did you hear that?" Cathy asked, turning around on the stepstool.

"Yeah...."

"Where is Tyler?"

I knew why she was asking about Tyler, because Tyler was the only beagle we had left that would play with the dog toys. Panda always acted like it was beneath her to play with dog toys. In fact, on many Christmas mornings, Panda would dig through her gifts, bypassing any toy and going straight for the treats. If you did happen to toss her a toy, the look on her face was priceless. The word "yuck" I think said it best. Panda hated putting anything into her mouth that did not have any nutritional value.

I got down from the ladder and found both Panda and Tyler asleep. I walked out of our bedroom and looked around the house downstairs. Then I went upstairs and found nothing. Not one thing could logically explain why both Cathy and I had heard a squeaky toy. Yes, I will admit our home has four full doggie toy boxes with some toys that squeak. However, none had ever squeaked on their own.

Then I remembered that, right after Penny's passing, one of our dear friends had said to us that it was her hope and prayer that Penny would find some way to let us both know she was okay. Was Penny simply trying, in her own way, to help Cathy and me heal? I really can't say. I only know that it did *not* feel eerie to us. Cathy and I welcomed those special times when they happened and missed them when they did not. Nonetheless, while I wish I could offer a logical and definitive answer for these happenings, I simply cannot.

Day by Day

*G*RIEF, HEALING AND CLOSURE are all words associated with death. Easy words to say. Nonetheless, for most anyone who has ever lost someone, or a pet, you know all too well that you will hear those words over and over again after a loss.

It has been my experience that we all handle death in our own unique way. Most importantly, we all handle it in our own time. While Cathy and I share many things—and I would go so far as to say we share many belief systems—we both approached the days after Penny's death from totally different sides. We were neither angry at each other nor upset with each other. We were different, and differences are okay; and, in many situations, they help create a balance. This was a life lesson we both learned after Gunner's passing. We had now learned the importance of the acceptance in allowing each other to grieve in our own way. Therefore, when Penny passed on, I allowed Cathy the space she needed to grieve while being there for her when she needed me. She offered me the same. However, after Penny's passing, we had some final arrangements to handle that we completed as one.

We agreed that we both wanted an impression of Penny's paw print taken. We had learned the hard way, after the loss of Gunner, to make this determination early. Finding out after the cremation is done that the impression has not been made, needless to say, is too late.

There are many options for pet owners today that are geared toward helping them with loss and closure and the uniqueness of that bond between the pet and human. Several days after Penny's passing, the facility that handled the arrangements called us to come down and take care of the final details. When we arrived, we were presented with Penny's clay paw impression along with a tiny bag. At first, both Cathy and I were taken aback as we looked at the contents within the tiny bag.

"I took the liberty of trimming a small amount of Penny's hair, and it is in the bag for you," the lady from the crematorium said, looking at Cathy and I. While we knew about the paw print, we had no idea about the hair; and we were both glad they had done this for us.

Next, Cathy wanted to pick out a pet urn. To Cathy, where Penny's ashes were to be kept was extremely important. For me, the ashes were simply part of the earthly body that Penny was in while here on earth, and with my belief system, Penny was no longer a part of that. So while the ashes had meaning to me, it was not quite the same as what Cathy felt.

I helped Cathy look through a booklet the lady offered us and offered my thoughts when Cathy asked for them. While all the urns were nice, none seemed to be fitting for Penny's final resting place, at least from Cathy's perspective. When we arrived home, Cathy took to the Internet looking at what was available. She made calls and sent emails by the dozens. Several days later, she came into my office and told me she had finally found what she felt was the right urn for Penny's ashes. Cathy had managed to find a wonderful place that provided a selection of hand-blown glass urns. I have to admit that, now, she was right. She was allowed to select such things as colors, size, and shape. With Penny in mind, she picked out an urn called Sacred Rainbow and, knowing Penny's signature color, she picked pink and colors that worked well with it.

While looking for the urn, Cathy managed to stumble across a place that provided handmade jewelry for inserting the pet's hair, which also preserved it. When she contacted the business, the woman requested that Cathy email her a photo of Penny. The jeweler told Cathy she always likes to have a photo of the pet while she is working on each individual piece.

I have to say everyone was both compassionate and very professional when dealing with Cathy and the loss of our Penny. While we know that all these things could never replace our wonderful beagle, Penny, in small ways, they help in the healing process. I for one was very grateful when the urn came in and we could finally put Penny's ashes to rest. To me, the important thing was having a resting place for the ashes. Although Cathy was glad that Penny's ashes were laid to rest, she was thankful that her ashes were not just in some box. To Cathy, the urn was a symbol of Penny's colors and life; and when the sunshine peeks through our living room window, the colors of blue and pink dance in a colorful arrangement that I think reminds all of us how much Penny loved the sun and blue skies. The urn also afforded us enough room to place one of her pink collars alongside her ashes.

Slowly and very gradually, things began to go back to some sense of normalcy. Day by day, little by little. Panda and Tyler, after three long weeks of mourning Penny's loss, began to come around. At first, knowing Penny and Panda were raised together from the time they were puppies, we feared we would lose Panda, too, from the grief Panda was suffering. However, just as the dawn breaks its magical spell to give way to a new day, Panda seemed to find it within herself to make that mental choice, which was to want to go on and move forward once again. Although both Tyler and Panda still had their moments when all they wanted was to be left alone and to sleep in their beds, going for walks and going for "bye-bye" soon became popular once again around our household with them both.

For me, I found that writing Penny's story had

a healing effect on me. My writing, however, did not have the same effect for Cathy.

As with everything I write, Cathy goes over it first before it ends up on the desk of my proof editor, Susan. When I started writing *Just this Side of Heaven*, Cathy read over the first few chapters as usual. However, as the book's journey inevitably led toward Penny's death, Cathy found that she could no longer read the words upon the pages. Furthermore, I found that when I read the words out loud to hear their flow upon the pages, it bothered both Panda and Tyler. The beagles who always loved to lie at my feet and be read to when I wrote suddenly would get up and leave my office in a state of depression. Therefore, I found myself making sure neither Cathy nor the beagles were within earshot of my reading. On several occasions, I pushed the manuscript away and started a new project, assuming that maybe I should not write Penny's story. Each time I did, I knew in my heart I had to finish.

It was then I realized I had another decision to make. Months before Penny's passing, book three in my children's book series, *Sleepytown Beagles, Oh Brother,* was sent to my publisher and was slated for release around fall or early winter. I had just finished the fourth book, *Sleepytown Beagles, Differences,* and had begun the fifth book in the series when Penny passed away. As I sat at my desk one day, I found myself faced with a dilemma—what do I do about Penny in the children's book series? After Cathy and I talked it over, we both agreed that Penny should live on within the pages of Sleepytown. Not only was she a wonderful character that taught kids all over the world lessons about life, but this also meant that part of her would always live on within the pages and in the hearts of kids of all ages, all over the world.

With that hurdle behind us, the weeks passed by, and Cathy and I began to give thought to the fact that both Penny and Panda shared the same biological parents. While they were a litter and nine months apart, the fact still remained that they had a shared genetic signature. Thus, the what-ifs began to surface within the shadows of our mind. Suddenly, we were faced with more questions than we had answers for. Could Panda also fall victim to the very disease that took Penny from us? When we first thought about this, we tried to shove those feelings aside. However, each time Panda would act the least bit different in anyway, both Cathy and I would worry. Calling our vet, we set up an appointment for Panda. She was given a complete physical along with a blood workup. When Dr. H. called a few days later, she said that Panda did not show any signs we had to worry about and that we should just enjoy the time we have with her.

Thoughts of Guilt

*A*FTER PENNY'S PASSING, along with the sorrow and pain of losing her, I have to admit, I felt a tremendous amount of guilt and even anger. While I know both Cathy and I did what we felt we had to do, somewhere deep within my own heart and mind, guilt was busy setting up shop along with its counterpart, anger. Oddly enough, I was unaware of this at first. It took many months after her death for me to even realize what was truly happening.

At first, it was simple fleeting thoughts that quickly passed through my mind like a car during rush hour, and then the thoughts became more pronounced, to the point where I would sit and ponder them for minutes at a time.

The reoccurring guilt thoughts were always the same. They were carbon copies of each other. One was as simple as this: I was the person who drove her to the to the veterinarian's office when we had to put her down that day in October. Another was a classic of my own persona, I like to call it my "what if" guilt thought. With this thought, I would always start by wondering, what if we would have waited just one more day, one more week, or tried one more bottle of medication. Would the outcome have been the same? While I know that type of thinking is truly a part of my own makeup, and know we had the very best vet in the world for Penny, logically, I know the outcome would not have changed. Nonetheless, before I could get a grip on my thoughts, I would find myself changing the scenario within the shadows of my mind. Like a picture puzzle, I found myself changing out the dates and events in an attempt to solve the unsolvable. The fact is, to have waited any longer would have sentenced Penny to more suffering.

The other guilt thought I refer to as my "good beagle parent" guilt thought. It went something like this: I would raise questions like, was I a good enough beagle dad to Penny? Did I get her the proper food? Did I provide enough exercise? Trust me, the list goes on and on. I found out months later that Cathy and I shared the same feelings of anger, which caused us to think, how in the world was this deadly thing growing inside of Penny and we did not realize it?

However, once I realized that guilt and anger were festering away within me. I quickly analyzed the feelings for what they really were. The fact is, no amount of second-guessing was going to change the outcome. Therefore, I had to realize that this was negative energy, and doing something more productive would be a better use of my time.

I think that, for the most part, each pet lover in the world who suffers a loss will go through these feelings to some degree. I believe it is important to first acknowledge that these feelings may exist. Allow yourself time to think about the feelings and thoughts; however, recognize guilt and don't allow it to overtake your life.

In my case, I know deep within my heart that I did everything humanly possible for our Penny. While I wish the outcome could have been different, I know there was nothing Cathy or I could have done to change the end result.

Therefore, I fought the guilt and anger with logic and knowledge. That isn't to say that on a bright spring day, when I step out into our backyard, taking in all the beautiful flowers and their aroma, I don't find myself longing to see Penny basking in her ray of sunshine. I know it is times like these that those sneaky thoughts of guilt and anger can creep into my mind so easily and without warning. Therefore, I have learned to replace those negative thoughts with positive ones.

Shadows and Memories

*T*ODAY, AS THE long days of winter relinquish their chill and colorless palette to a bright spring day full of beautiful sunshine that warms the earth, I walk as I have always done. I enjoy the various shades of pink from the purple leaf plums that line the streets in bloom before they leaf out for summer. Walking my beagles as a daily routine has not changed, other than the void I feel deep down inside from the loss of Penny. Many times, Cathy or I will still pick up one of Penny's collars and hook it on our belt as we take the other two beagles for a walk.

Nonetheless, my comfort comes when the sun is to my back, Tyler is on my right, and Panda is on my left. As I look downward and to my left, I see a shadowy image just beyond Panda, as if this shadowy beagle is leading the way on our journey. My logical mind reasons that this is simply Panda's shadow stretched out before her. Also, the lack of a complete shadow in front of Tyler could only be explained as the angle from the sun's rays. Nonetheless, I feel Penny's presence during these times, and it touches my heart deeply. It is during my solitary walks, minus any human being to clutter my thoughts, that I tell her how much she is missed and loved by all who had the opportunity and blessing to know her. Then, just as quickly as the shadow appears, it is gone once again. And I know she is just this side of heaven.

Epilogue

*I*N CLOSING, I WANT TO leave you with a few things to think about. That is, life here on this earth is first and foremost a gift to each of us. It does not matter if that life walks this earth on two legs or four. What does matter is the way we approach each day we are given to share our gift of life. Life does not provide us with a rewind button—we will never get back yesterday; but today, each and every one of us can make a difference in our life, as well as in the lives of others. And yet, tomorrow is only a promise, not a guarantee.

All too often, I believe, and this is only my opinion, we deal with death as the end, which, in a way, it is, but only here on this earth. We are born and take on an earthly form. However, I truly believe in my heart that Penny's death was not the end. Rather, she ceased to exist in the earthly form that others and I came to know and love. I feel she earned the right to passage beyond this world into another world we have yet to experience. That said, I understand all too well that what we cannot see in today's society is hard for us to fathom and buy into. Thus, acceptance of death here on this earth is hard for many to understand.

I will continue to hold dear to my heart the promise of a life even better than what you or I know as our earthly existence today. Therefore, I choose to celebrate Penny's life. I look at it in this way: God blessed me with this wonderful beagle and the time we had to share was a gift. While I may not have been ready for, nor wanted Penny to leave that Friday evening in October, it was Penny's time to move on beyond this world.

It is my hope and desire that with this tribute to Penny, she will once again teach people about life and also about living. With that said, I choose to believe death is not a goodbye; rather, it's a difference.

While my feelings about death help me, there

is still a sense of loss, of something missing, a deep void, and I embrace that for what that is to me. I miss so many things about Penny and the other beagles I have loved and lost. Nevertheless, the loss does not go away. However, I do things that I think will help in the healing process. For example, there are days when either Cathy or I will grab Penny's collar and latch it on to our belts when we take the other beagles out on our walks. In March 2008, when Cathy and I took Panda and Tyler on a road trip from Albuquerque to Durango, Colorado, there on the rearview mirror was Penny's collar. The collar is symbolic of things that help us see what we can no longer see as humans. As we go about our daily lives here on this earth, Penny has not been forgotten, and never will be.

Many friends have asked when we will get another beagle. Today is just too soon for us to even think about it. However, yesterday was a reminder once again that Panda is reaching her golden years. As Cathy and I walked Panda and Tyler, Panda made it halfway around the block and could not finish the walk. As Cathy and Tyler went on to finish their walk, I stood with Panda as she watched them leave, and I could see how badly she wanted to continue but just could not. I reached down and scooped her up into my arms. I carried her the rest of the way home, cradled in my arms. As we walked by ourselves on the shortcut to our home, I talked with her and showed her things as I always do with the beagles on our walks. It wasn't until I opened our front door and removed her leash that the tears filled my eyes.

About the Author

TIMOTHY GLASS was born in Pennsylvania and moved to the southwest with his family as a child. Tim graduated from the University of New Mexico. He spent some time in New England and now lives in Albuquerque, New Mexico. More than 300 of his nonfiction articles have been published nationally and internationally. He is currently working on several writing projects, including the popular Sleepytown Beagles series. He is also a staff writer for a global monthly newsletter put out by OurDogHouse.com. Tim is also writing a new novel titled *Postcards*. Tim enjoys the company of his wife, Cathy, and his tri-colored beagles. He also enjoys camping, hiking, weight training, and woodworking. He is a member of the Author's Guild of America, Author's League of America, and past member of IEEE Computer Society.

CPSIA information can be obtained at www.ICGtesting.com
Printed in the USA
LVOW12s0832040813

346134LV00001B/63/P